EDWARD DART

1922 — 1975

EDWARD DART
ARCHITECT

❧

SUSAN DART

EVANSTON PUBLISHING
EVANSTON, ILLINOIS 60202

EVANSTON PUBLISHING, INC.
1216 HINMAN AVENUE
EVANSTON, IL 60202

Library of Congress Preassigned Catalog Number:
93-070276

Printed in the USA
All Rights Reserved

10 9 8 7 6 5 4 3 2 1

ISBN: 1-879260-09-3

CONTENTS

ACKNOWLEDGMENTS

It is impossible to list all the people who helped in this endeavor. But it would be equally impossible for me not to mention some who were especially helpful. Besides family members—my sister and brother, Ninette and Harry Dart, and my sister-in-law, Wilma Dart, all of whom provided facts and pictures and reminiscences, there are those outside the family who loved Ned enough to interrupt their busy lives to help.

First among these is Father Michael Komechak, a careful and competent art historian, who provided facts, photos, and most of the information for the lists of buildings.

In addition, help from the following people was invaluable: Arthur Miller at Lake Forest College; Mildred Martin Buster of Lexington, KY; Mary Daley, Ned's secretary; Kenan Heise of the *Chicago Tribune;* and George Jones, who performed meticulous word processing.

For help with photography: Jana Brinton; Richard Cutler, who rephotographed all the old pictures and took many of the new ones; Ann Duncan; Joseph Lucas; Ken Miles; Paul Myers; Claude Peck; Sylvia Preston; and Barbara Wood-Prince, who did a complete photographic study of our house before it was demolished.

For help with French translation and accents, Franklin and Marie-Odile Sweetser.

Among the architects who gave their time and expertise are Laurence Booth, Sheldon Hill, Anne McCutcheon Lewis, Carter Manny, Edward Straka, Stanley Tigerman, and John Vinci.

I'm grateful to the Graham Foundation for Advanced Studies in the Fine Arts for its support. And I'm especially grateful to my husband, John McCutcheon, who as always, was willing to lend his editorial ability—and his support—whenever I needed it. And I needed it often.

Susan Dart
Lake Forest, Illinois
1993

CHAPTER ONE

❧

EARLY DAYS

The astonishing thing about my brother, Edward Dart, is how unlikely he was to succeed. If you had lined up the Dart children when we were growing up, there's no doubt where Ned, as we called him, would have come—last, or more likely not even in the running.

There were four of us who survived infancy. Harry, with his exceptionally brilliant mind, and Ninette, who won the citizenship prize in grade school and was fluent in French, were the two oldest. I was next and according to my teachers (who were, alas, dead wrong), I had a promising career ahead in art or singing. It was these same teachers who shook their heads in despair over Ned. He was a disruptive nuisance, and though they laughed at his antics and loved him for making them laugh, it was clear they thought he would never amount to anything. They were dead wrong about him too.

As it turned out Ned was successful beyond anything they—or we—could have imagined. He was listed in *Who's Who in America,* which none of the rest of us were, and received more honors and awards than anyone can count. His habit seems to have been to stash away the certificates and scrolls in a drawer and forget about them—or more likely throw them away as was his custom with his drawings when he was done with them. But even without an accurate list of his honors, not to mention a complete list of his buildings, it's easy to find dozens of citations and newspaper encomiums about him and his work.

For example, the American Institute of Architects (AIA) alone gave him eighteen awards, one of which was the AIA National Honor Award.

He was made a fellow of the AIA, one of the highest honors that organization can bestow, when he was only 44, and the citations and honors from other organizations are so numerous that they become repetitive. Phrases like the following abound: "the jury commended the pleasant adaptation of the building to its site"; "outstanding religious architecture"; "expert handling of space"; "the jury particularly admired the play of volume against volume"; "an orderly relation of plans and elevations"; "poetic"; "a kind of vigor and vitality"; and so on.

Altogether he worked on about two hundred projects, over a hundred of which were completed—all by the time he was 53 and just reaching the peak of his powers. He was also just beginning to get really big commissions for buildings such as the cancer center of the King Faisal Hospital in Saudi Arabia and Water Tower Place in Chicago.

Water Tower Place, one of the tallest buildings in Chicago at the time, was the world's tallest reinforced concrete building. It was the first mixed-use building under one roof—over three million square feet. Although condemned at first by the critics, it was to become, like Ned himself, a success beyond anyone's expectations. Among the people it was one of Chicago's best liked buildings from the start. It still is.

But Ned's most important contribution was the influence that he had on architecture and is sure to have again in the future. "The sooner the better," an architectural historian told me recently. "The profession has sunk so low that it has lost respect. Much of what passes for architecture today is tinsel. It's fake. Some of it is downright crazy. Then we look at what Dart stood for—the clarity of his work, the honesty, and we know that this is what we must emulate. That is why his work is being studied again." Author and historian Kenan Heise of the *Chicago Tribune* sums it up. "Ed Dart," he says, "made a nudge in the world."

His story begins in New Orleans, Louisiana, on May 28, 1922. I was two years old when he was born, and of course I don't remember the day, but he was born like all the rest of us at home. He was christened Edouard Dupaquier Dart but was called Ned from the beginning, and though when he was grown he wanted to be called Ed, all of us who knew him early on still refer to him as Ned.

As to Edouard he would have none of it. Even as late as the 1920s, there was still a distinction in New Orleans between the "French" and the "Americans," the one meaning people of French ancestry, who spoke French in their homes, and the other meaning everybody else, who spoke English. We were half French and half American. Kids hate to be different, and though in New Orleans the French influence was and still is strong, French names like ours were something—if not to be ashamed of—at least to avoid. Ned anglicized his name to Edward just as I changed mine from Suzanne Micheline to Susan.

Ned was the fourth of five children. Harry, whose full name was Henry Plauché Dart III, was born in 1917 in a small rented house on Freret Street, but by the time my sister, Ninette (Eugénie Louise Dart),

The Dart family just before Roger's birth.
Mother, Dad, Ninette, Ned, Susan, Harry

came along, our parents had moved into a new and more commodious house on the corner of Adams Street and South Claiborne Avenue in New Orleans. Whether they had an architect design the house for them or whether it was already built is unknown. Ninette was born there in 1918. I was born there in 1920, then Ned, then Roger in 1924. We were all two years or less apart, and though it was grand for us kids, it was hell for our parents, especially our mother.

She had little or no domestic help, and although her parents, Grand-mère and Grand-père Dupaquier, lived next door—and Grand-père was a doctor—the burden of caring for five children rested on her shoulders. They spoke French among themselves and though we couldn't understand what they were saying, we knew from the tone that she was often near the breaking point. Nor could it have been easy for our father, considering the way he had been brought up. Even the house was not to their taste.

Still standing at 2410 Adams Street, four blocks from Carrollton Avenue, it is a two-story frame house. It is somewhat more cheerful looking today with its coat of white paint, but in our day it was painted a gloomy brown and had hardly any trees around it. The main entrance was on Adams Street up a half flight of concrete steps to a landing with more steps to the right leading to a screened porch which in turn led directly into a dark, wainscoted living room. The entire living quarters were on that floor, resulting in what is known in New Orleans as a raised cottage. With the basement at ground level and high ceilinged rooms above, this sort of raised house is sensible in the hot, humid climate in New Orleans and has long been popular.

There are many beautiful examples of raised cottages in Louisiana, especially the Greek revival ones with their gracious columns, wide porches (called galleries), and recessed doorways. You can still see any number of these in the Garden District in New Orleans, a section of the city developed in the pre-Civil War boom days of 1830-1860.

Unfortunately, our house, built right after World War I, was not in that league. It was, as Ned was later to characterize such structures, "building, not architecture." He was also to say that growing up in New Orleans, where its range in architecture swings from the best to the worst,

2410 Adams Street as it looks today

was one of the most profound influences on his work. Our house, though not beautiful, was sturdily built.

And as Grand-mère pointed out complacently and frequently—their house next door was also a raised house—these two houses were practical. "Confortable," she would say, pronouncing it as if she were speaking French, and "pratique." She was right. The basement, in our house as well as hers, was a grand place to play. We had tricycles, roller skates, an old baby buggy, and a wonderful stuffed bear on wheels that Dad (we called him Daddy then) had brought us from one of his trips to New York.

Outside we had a plain rectangular lawn unencumbered by trees and a long sidewalk along South Claiborne to play on. Both Adams Street and South Claiborne were unpaved, and an open drainage ditch for rainwater ran down the middle of South Claiborne Avenue, which like most of what are called avenues in New Orleans was a wide divided street. In New Orleans almost all divided streets bear the designation "avenue," or sometimes "boulevard," to distinguish them from plain streets. There are exceptions but the only ones I can think of off hand are Palmer Avenue, which is not divided, and Canal Street, which is. But whereas most avenues have a landscaped neutral ground down the middle, ours had only streetcar tracks next to a steep embankment leading to the drainage ditch, or canal as we called it, far below. We were forbidden to go down to the canal, but we could go almost anywhere else we wanted, so our neighborhood was not an unhappy place for children—it was just raw and new and not beautiful.

The Dupaquier house next door, still standing at 7719 South Claiborne, was similar to ours. Built at about the same time, it was partly of wood and partly of a rough, dark red brick. The wood was stained a practical but morbid brownish-red, and heavy duty concrete steps led up to a screened porch and thence to the front door, which like ours led directly into the living room. Whether our grandparents built or bought the house I don't know, but a consideration such as an inviting entrance hall would never have occurred to Grand-mère, who undoubtedly had been in charge of whatever housing choices were made. Grand-père was a scientist and a scholar and did not concern himself with such things.

7719 S. Claiborne, Grand-mère and Grand-père's house, 1920s

Dupaquier house as it looks today

Grand-mère had little interest in aesthetics, which was odd because in her background were people of some artistic achievement. Her father had been a maker of gold chalices in France before he came to America with a certificate from the bishop of Valence attesting to his skill. We still have the certificate, dated 1855. He never used it because when he arrived in New Orleans he found a sluggish market for gold chalices and went into the grocery business instead. By good luck, or more probably by hard work, he did well. This was a good thing because his wife, Grand-mère's mother, insisted on going to Paris regularly for her hats and dresses and perfumed soap while he would take the waters at Vichy.

They were long dead by the time we came along, and in any case their elegant-sounding habits had not rubbed off on Grand-mère. Her greatest happiness was her home and her family. "Woman's place is in the home," she used to say contentedly, and even then, though I loved her, I didn't buy her philosophy. She had no regular servant that I can remember and did all her own cooking, chopping off the heads of the chickens she cooked, plucking them, and making the best stewed chicken you ever tasted—not to mention homemade noodles and cakes and a heavenly white confection called divinity fudge. She didn't care a bit about the kind of house she lived in or the kind of clothes she wore as long as they were clean and, above all, "confortable."

It may have been an unstylish way of life, the neighborhood may have lacked the charm of the old established New Orleans neighborhoods, and the houses may have been unlovely, but largely because of Grand-mère and Grand-père, ours was a secure, happy childhood. You can, after all, learn from ugliness as well as from beauty, and by the time we were grown we had learned to love beautiful things.

I remember a funny incident. Grand-mère loved to take the streetcar downtown to Canal Street, and she especially loved to take one or two of us children with her and let us pick out something to wear. Grand-père bought us trinkets, but Grand-mère, ever the practical one, bought us clothes or shoes. One day she took Ned and me downtown to buy Ned a suit. He must have been about four, and when the saleslady displayed the suits in his size, he latched on to one with bright green pants and a top of loud black and green checks with shiny black buttons that held the pants to the shirt. I was already old enough to know this was an unfortunate choice, but he insisted. Grand-mère said, "If that's what he wants, that is what he shall have." Always eager to make children happy, she thought it was okay. But even the saleslady looked distressed. I can remember Mother's comment when we got home. "Grand-mère," she muttered, "is foolish to waste money that way." But Ned loved that suit and wore it until he outgrew it, mostly around the house. It took years for him to acquire the excellent taste in clothes, not to mention other areas, for which he was to become known.

He wasn't in school yet, but Harry, Ninette, and I were. We were sent to St. Rita's parochial school a few blocks away. To understand why we were sent to St. Rita's requires some discussion of our religion and hence our ancestry, a subject I find boring when I read biographies of other people. I always want to get on with the person the book is about, not his or her forebears. Even in the hands of the most skillful authors, long lines of ancestors are hard to keep straight and too often get tangled in the reader's mind. To avoid that, and yet demonstrate that I did check out our ancestors as far back as I reasonably could, I've listed them in the Appendix, which you can skip if you choose.

On the other hand, some background is necessary, especially since Ned was later to build churches for many different denominations and was to become, in a way, a deeply spiritual person, though not in the conventional sense. I remember once in the 1950s when he was battling over architectural details with some church vestrymen, or elders, or whatever they were, his telling me privately that they were "the most un-Christian bastards" he had ever met. He was not pious.

❧

Maternal Ancestry

On our mother's side we were a hundred percent Latin. Her mother, Grand-mère Dupaquier, was born Eugénie Limongi in New Orleans in 1868. Grand-mère's father, the chalice maker, was an Italian who had moved to France before coming to America and settling in New Orleans. There he married Louise Saillard, a native New Orleanean from whose French ancestors she must have inherited her fancy taste in perfumed soap and Paris dresses. It was she, you'll recall, who liked to go to Paris for her clothes and toiletries.

Mother's father, Grand-père Dupaquier, was all French, his people having emigrated from France in the middle of the nineteenth century when times were particularly hard in Europe and particularly good in New Orleans—thanks largely to the cotton boom which lasted until the

Civil War broke the back of the south. These maternal ancestors of ours, though bilingual, spoke French exclusively in their homes, were well educated, hard working, and of course, Catholics. None of them moved away from the French Quarter, or Vieux Carré, until Mother's marriage to Dad in 1915.

Grand-père's parents, like Grand-mère's, were well-off and well-educated. Grand-père's father, Dr. Auguste Dupaquier, was a skillful and successful physician. His French passport, preserved all these years, shows that he came to America at age 16 in 1853 with his family, whose belief in freedom was a factor in their emigration. They prospered and were able to send Auguste to St. Louis, Missouri, to medical school. So firmly had the belief in freedom been instilled in the young Dr. Auguste and so great was his self-assurance that during the Civil War when the emancipation of slaves was proclaimed he proudly flew the Union flag at his front door. This was during the Yankee occupation of the city and he was reviled by his Confederate neighbors for siding with the enemy. But his practice apparently did not suffer because in 1873 he sent his oldest son, Edouard Dupaquier, our grandfather, to be educated in Paris.

This young boy, age fourteen, went all alone to Sainte-Barbe, a lycée that still exists. He was bright and hard-working and pursued his education in Paris for 12 years without once returning home. He went on to the Université de Paris (the Sorbonne) where he got two degrees, the bachelor of arts and the bachelor of science.

Just as he was about to enter medical school in 1880, his father was killed in New Orleans (possibly in a duel—reportedly over a lady) leaving no money. Edouard, age twenty-two, stayed on in Paris anyhow and received his medical degree in 1885. He earned his own way by tutoring young Englishmen in the French language—Englishmen, Grand-mère told us years later, whom he looked upon as frivolous. You can well imagine why.

Here was this newly poor New Orleanean all alone in Paris, so hungry he sometimes ate roasted rats in his garret—here he was tutoring rich English boys in a language they could easily have picked up for themselves. He, after all, had picked up Latin and Greek, not to mention Spanish and Italian, and was dabbling in Esperanto. I believe Grand-mère's account of the Latin and Greek and Esperanto (I found books of his in those languages in the attic), but I'm not so sure about the roasted rats. Grand-mère liked a colorful story.

Anyhow he stuck it out, paying his way through his entire training at the Faculté de Médecine de Paris. Even as a student he began to attract attention. He studied under Dr. Pierre Paul Emile Roux, right hand man to Louis Pasteur, the world famous bacteriologist to whom the world owes much of its knowledge of germs and to whom Ned and the rest of us Dart children owed our lives, as we shall see later in this story. Grand-père kept up with Dr. Roux and his work in immunology, which stood him in good stead later in his own practice.

In 1885, after receiving his Diplôme de Docteur en Médecine, he returned to New Orleans ready to support his now impoverished mother

Edouard Dupaquier as a boy

13

and orphaned sister. His brothers had already struck out for themselves in modest occupations—one ran a dairy and another a candy-making business. I'm sorry to say that we never kept up with the descendants of these other family members.

In late 1886, a year and a half after returning to New Orleans, the young Dr. Dupaquier wrote a letter in French, which we still have, to M. and Mme. Limongi. These were the parents of a young lady, ten years his junior, whom he had not known before he went away, though the families were acquainted with one another. In the most delicate way he asks if he may become better acquainted with the seventeen-year-old "Mademoiselle Eugénie" and hints, but clearly, that if she is not displeased, he plans to marry her. The letter gives a good idea of what kind of people they were: "We have the same tastes, the same ideas," he says, "We are of the same good hard-working bourgeois class, intelligent, sober, this bourgeoisie that leads the world today."

Mlle. Eugénie was not displeased. They were married on February 4, 1887, and his love for her, undemonstrative but sure, was matched by her devotion to him. I never heard a cross word between them.

Their first house was a small one, no longer standing, on the other side of North Rampart Street from the French Quarter. He had his medical office in his house and went about on foot to his patients. Their first child, Suzanne Angèle Dupaquier, our mother, was born in that house on June 20, 1888. Soon thereafter they moved to 819 Orleans Street, only a block or two from St. Louis Cathedral. The house was new, or almost new, when they bought it—a sturdily built house that is still in good condition today.

Grand-père's office was in the first room on the left as you enter the front door. The dining room was behind the office and the kitchen behind that. The bedrooms were on the right side of the house, and outside on the left was a narrow driveway leading to a rear courtyard where there was a stable for Grand-père's horse and buggy and living quarters for his faithful servant, Arthur. It is all there today except for the stable in the rear which burnt down some years ago. I went there with Mother a few years before she died and she remembered everything.

Grand-mère and Grand-père's house
819 Orleans Street (1988 photo)

Grand-père did well in his profession. Though he never became rich he did become one of New Orleans' most respected physicians and was president of the Orleans Parish Medical Society from 1906 to 1917. Having studied abroad, as few other doctors had, he kept up with the medical advances there as well as in the United States. Thanks to his acquaintance with Dr. Roux, who developed the diphtheria antitoxin, Grand-père was the first physician in New Orleans—in 1888—to inoculate people against that disease. "Children were dying by the hundreds of diphtheria, especially in the poor Italian Quarter, and he never turned down anyone," Mother told me. "He would charge only fifty cents for a house call if the family was poor, and he sometimes left a dollar or two on the mantle when he saw real need."

It was the same during the yellow fever epidemics. He was always willing to go to the homes of the dying, and every day he took the long drive in his buggy to the quarantine camp, which was about where the New Orleans Country Club is today.

Edouard Michel Dupaquier
Grand-père (1915 photo)

Eugénie Limongi Dupaquier
Grand-mère (1915 photo)

Few of his fellow doctors would venture even to the poor parts of town, let alone the quarantine camp, thinking that yellow fever was spread by contact with victims. Though he did not know any more than they what caused yellow fever, he went anyhow. It was not until the culprit, the *Aëdes aegypti mosquito,* was discovered that the disease was defeated mostly by eradicating their breeding places.

By the time we children came along and Grand-mère and Grand-père had moved uptown, most of the dreadful tropical diseases were no longer a threat. The last yellow fever epidemic had been in 1905, and except for the usual childhood diseases we were a healthy lot, and our unstylish neighborhood a salubrious place to grow up.

But St. Rita's parochial school was not salubrious—not for us anyway. Harry, Ninette, and I were sent there because Dad never interfered with Mother's religion. In fact, he always encouraged us to do whatever she asked and even went to Mass with the family once or twice. He was a Methodist but attended church only rarely. Grand-mère and Grand-père, though nominally Catholics, never went to church that I can remember, nor did they follow any of the church rules such as fasting during Lent or not eating meat on Friday, which in those days was a grave sin. Mother, possibly to balance all this indifference, became, if not a militant, at least a slavishly obedient Catholic. When the time came, we were sent to St. Rita's parochial school.

My Catholic friends today tell me the church has changed—that love, not sin is the dominant theme, but it is hard to erase the perceptions of childhood. Ned did not attend St. Rita's school, nor was he compelled to go to Mass at St. Rita's Church every Sunday or to make his first confession and first communion there as Harry, Ninette, and I did, so his feeling toward the Church was more forgiving than mine.

A large red-faced priest was in charge of the whole parish, and on Sundays he gave thundering sermons on hell and damnation, his red face growing redder as he warmed to his subject.

In the school the nuns in their black habits with their cardboard-stiff bibs and heavy wooden rosaries jangling like jailers' keys from their waists, took up where he left off, and by the time we got home we were trembling. Ninette, who wasn't as callous as Harry or I, was frequently in tears.

One of the nuns had a favorite book which she read in installments to the older children, older being third and fourth graders. It was a detailed study of hell, and though I heard it second hand from Ninette, I remember it vividly. I also remember the distinct implication that all of us kids were headed straight in that direction.

The gates of hell, I recall picturing them in my childish mind, were so hot that the hinges were melting and flames were leaping through the bars. The gatekeeper, whose fun was just beginning, would open the gates and scrape his latest customers in. In one installment there would be ovens into which he'd pop his victims and in another it would be a fiery uphill road that people had to climb barefoot only to reach an even hotter place, etc. etc. I had nightmares from which I'd awaken screaming.

Even though the very youngest children were spared this now incredible form of instruction, we nevertheless had to form ranks and march into the dismal classrooms where a ruler was frequently banged on the teacher's desk (never on us, thank goodness) to make us pay attention. I was in a class called Low Primer, and though I went to St. Rita's for a couple of years, I don't believe I was ever promoted to High Primer. I was so shaken all the time that I couldn't learn to read, and I was made to feel it was somehow my fault.

Too young for school, Ned meanwhile stayed home and played, and I missed him. I think he missed us too because whenever Ninette and I played our favorite game ("let's play like we're ladies"), he was always willing—even eager—to be the husband or son or whatever the scenario called for—sometimes the dog.

In the meanwhile there was another strong influence in our lives, although none of us realized at the time just how strong and how good it was. I'm ashamed that it took so long for us to understand this. It was our paternal heritage.

⋎

Paternal Ancestry

Our grandfather Dart lived about two miles away in a fine white house at 1904 Palmer Avenue, a few blocks from St. Charles Avenue. The house is still standing and is still fairly elegant. For us in the 1920s it might as well have been on a different planet. How we hated going there, but we had to go call on Grandpa Dart every Sunday—or what I remember as every Sunday. It was probably more like one Sunday out of four. In any case, we were scrubbed and dressed to the nines, and with our parents, whom we called at the time Mamma and Daddy (we changed to Mother, or Mom, and Dad when we were older and more sophisticated), we trooped out to the streetcar stop on South Claiborne Avenue, transferring at Carrollton, still one of the ugliest intersections in New Orleans.

Ned, Ninette, Harry, Susan, and Roger all dressed up to visit Grandpa Dart

Can you picture it? A handsome, patient man, a thin, tired-looking woman, and five little kids, the boys dressed in white sailor suits and the girls in pink organdy, on a streetcar, even then a plebeian form of transportation. Mother told me years later that other passengers sometimes used to snicker at us and make remarks. It was then, I am sure, that I determined I'd never have a large family.

Anyhow here's what happened Sunday after Sunday—or however often it was. We'd arrive at Grandpa Dart's house on Palmer Avenue, and the door would be opened by a pale-skinned black maid in a black uniform, a white apron, edged with a ruffle, and a matching white headband on her head. Grandpa Dart's unmarried daughters, Aunt May, Aunt Sally, and I guess Aunt Edith before she married and moved into a house of her own, were always on hand. I never heard their father call them by name; he called them "daughter." They ushered us into a room where Grandpa Dart sat in state in a big chair and we each went up and greeted him. We may have shaken his hand—for a while Ninette and I had to curtsey—but I know we never kissed him. I don't remember that he ever got up when we arrived, though he did sometimes see us to the door when we left.

Everyone deferred to him while we sat or stood rigidly answering his questions about the books we had read and fascinating topics like that. I don't recall one instance of affection or humor or fun on his part—not even warmth. After a while we were let loose to play in the yard, and though anything was better than sitting in that room with him, there wasn't much we could do outdoors. There were no swings or toys, and in our fancy clothes, what kind of outdoor games could we play? Since the morning had been ruined by having to go to church and the afternoon by having to go to Grandpa Dart's, the entire day was shot. These visits continued—less frequently, to be sure —until he died in 1934. They were a blight on our lives.

The tragedy is that they shouldn't have been. Grandpa Dart was a brilliant man—kind and generous, upright, noble of spirit, and yes, sensitive and loving. I never really got to know him until after he died and only then by reading the innumerable things written by and about him. Whose fault it was that his true self was hidden from us I'll never discover.

It was probably just circumstances. It may have been bitterness over his early life, or it may have been partly Mother's doing because she hated pomposity and she hated kowtowing even more. In any case, now that I know what he really was like under his formidable exterior, I'd give anything to have known him better.

He came from good stock: English on his father's side, French on his mother's. His father, Henry Dart, was of an ancient Devonshire family (witness place names like Dartmouth and Dartmoor). In 1837, at age 30, this first Henry Dart emigrated from England and settled in Louisiana. He was an engineer and a surveyor, who moved from place to place as jobs came up—jobs such as surveying for the railroad and superintending the construction of bridges and buildings. This Henry Dart (Grandpa's father) married Mary Plauché, whose father, Jacques Urbain Plauché, had served as aide-de-camp to General Andrew Jackson at the Battle of New Orleans. (His brother was the famous major, later general, Jean Baptiste Plauché who was in charge of the New Orleans troops.)

Henry and Mary Plauché Dart, had ten children, of whom the first six died early, possibly because of the many moves to primitive out-of-the-way places as he went from job to job. Their seventh child was my grandfather, Henry Plauché Dart. He was born in Fort St. Philip, Louisiana in 1858 while his father was superintending construction in progress at the fort. He was the first white child born there.

By the time the civil war broke out in 1861 the family was living in New Orleans. The shattered economy and the devastation that followed, during what is ironically called reconstruction, deeply affected my grandfather's life and in turn ours. He was forced by his father to leave school and go to work, something for which Grandpa Dart never forgave his father. Here was a boy, bright and eager, thirsting for knowledge, singled out as a born scholar by his teachers; and yet in spite of his entreaties, he was made to quit when he finished elementary school and go to work.

In an unpublished autobiography he wrote much later in life, when he was in his fifties, he tells of his early days. As the family fortune declined after the war, they moved to ever smaller houses, mostly in the area around Napoleon Avenue and the river. He went to the public schools in whatever ward they were in until he was ten or eleven when he switched to a school in another ward, which he says was "a fortunate change and marks the first era of my life."

> The principal was Mrs. Rosina Davis, a woman of great character... Under her I received all the schooling I ever got... I leaped mentally... She used to invite a choice few of her scholars to come to see her. Her house had several attractions, chiefly books, and I remember that it was her copy of Carlyle's *French Revolution* that first introduced me to that author.
> Aside from these things, there was nothing in my boyhood in the line of idle pleasure, save the ball games which we used to play during recess.

But even that was over. Mrs. Davis tried hard to see that he continue in school ("I was her prize scholar"), but his father's mind was made up. "This then," he ironically concludes the section on his schooling, "was the daylight and sunshine and happiness of my early days."

Adversity, however, was a goad towards success. In December, 1871, age 13, he answered a help wanted ad for work in a men's clothing store. With only a dime for the round trip carfare and no lunch, he went to the store and was put to work immediately behind a high desk as cashier.

"I had never seen money in any quantity, and had never counted any large sum," he says of his first day. "Here I was instantly thrust into a duty where every moment I was receiving money from a half score of employees and had to keep count of it. I still remember that first long day away from home. I was hungry and homesick and my duties only ended at midnight. I was to be paid $10.00 per month."

He was not a quitter—then or ever. Nor was he insensitive: "The first money I drew was $1.10 which I gave to my mother to buy a calico dress for herself and which she, dear soul, bought at my desire."

He stayed at that job, that "cheap slave camp," for a year. Then he got another job as delivery boy for a wholesale notions business that dealt with hundreds of little stores all over the city. This job gave him, if not a higher salary, at least a lot of good outdoor exercise and a thorough knowledge of New Orleans, which was to stand him in good stead later.

Sometime during his first year he was entrusted to go downtown to Exchange Place between Canal and Customhouse Streets to pay his parents' rent. This mission was to change his life.

"I walked for the first time in my life into a lawyer's office. It was May 6, 1872 in the morning. The lawyer was busy and I was told to sit down." He had never heard of lawyers or the law before— "it was a new word in my vocabulary." But he knew about books, and the walls were lined with them.

It so happened they needed an office boy and young Dart, eager and trustworthy, was asked if he wanted the job. "It was as though I had suddenly been let into heaven," he says.

His job required plenty of writing (this was before the introduction of typewriters and stenographers who took shorthand) and plenty of reading.

On his first day he was given the first volume of Kent's *Commentaries* to read and, he says, "a great, wide, splendid world was opening before my fourteen-year-old eyes. I swore to be a lawyer—to be a lawyer like the great ones."

He stayed in that law office for seven years, working hard and learning mightily. "I had the opportunity to read and I read omnivorously: law, literature, politics, everything that was in print... I read the court reports ... and the two codes at least a dozen times. In the line of duty I copied, and as I grew older, helped to prepare all sorts of pleadings and cases."

In the end, he received a thorough grounding in the law, not to mention wide experience and knowledge. He wanted more than ever to be a lawyer, but to be admitted to the bar in those days required passing two rigorous oral examinations. One was before a committee of lawyers in the clerk's office of the Supreme Court of Louisiana, and the following day another in court with the Chief Justice presiding. It was a grueling test for one who had had no formal legal training—indeed, no formal education at all beyond grammar school.

"I said nothing to anybody as the time approached for the committee meeting, and one cold stormy night in February, 1879, went quietly down to the clerk's office of the Supreme Court."

The session that night was "lengthy and searching," but Dart, answered the questions so well that at one point two of the lawyers got into a heated debate between themselves over his definition of homicide. "At last," he says, "toward eleven o'clock Labat [one of the lawyers] said he desired to ask me some questions on Justinian. The character of the examination, which had exhausted the usual questions, may be judged by this; I told him I had Cooper's edition near me on the table and that I had been reviewing it in the car down. That broke down the Committee's patience and they adjourned.

"I reached home that night at 12 midnight and found my mother and father sitting in the warm kitchen awaiting my return. I can see them now, dear old people, and how bright their faces grew as I assured them the worst was over." But he knew there was still one more hurdle—the examination before the Chief Justice, which would take place the next afternoon.

He had to go to work anyhow and slipped out just in time for the exam. A fellow candidate was examined first. They grilled him mercilessly, and finally turned him down with the usual advice to return later. "Then I went up."

As Dart approached the bench, two of the five justices stood up. They bowed and left the room.

> I felt my heart sink. Then the Chief Justice nodded to DeBlanc who proceeded to put a hypothetical case concerning the fixing of boundaries. It required more than the usual short reply and I restated the question and answered it. Then DeBlanc nodded to Spencer who shook his head and looked at the Chief Justice and out of his mouth came something which in my anxious state I thought was a question. I begged him to repeat it and he, with a tired, bored face, replied in a deep growl, "I said, step around here and be sworn in." In a moment the clerk was administering the oath and my seven years of apprenticeship was over.

He was 21. He reported back to work at 4:30 to the black looks of his boss for having been away from the office so long.

He didn't learn until thirty-three years later why the two justices had walked out and why his examination had been so brief. One of the examiners from the night before had reported to the court how brilliantly he had done, which rendered the court examination a mere formality and thus did not require any lengthy questioning or the presence of the entire bench. He also learned that Judge DeBlanc had spoken in high terms of the perfect answer he had given to his question. Dart's star was in the ascendancy.

Not long thereafter, on September 28, 1880, he opened his own office and soon after that another dream began to come true. Two years earlier he had met a beautiful and brilliant young woman, Mary Lytle Kernan, daughter of Judge William F. Kernan of Clinton, Louisiana. That family was so far above his socially that meeting her in the first place was entirely fortuitous. Here, in his words, is how it happened.

> One day in 1877, there walked into the office [the law office where he had started as an office boy five years earlier] a tall handsome blond, with a cheery voice inquiring for Plauché Dart. He had been sent with the recommendation that I could prepare him for a bar examination which he had come down from the country to take. This was my introduction to Thomas Jones Kernan, whom I liked from the start and who took an equally violent fancy to me. That introduction was one of the events of my life, for to it I owe my wife and all that that meant.
>
> Kernan was one of those men who took the world by the hand without fear and who in turn the world seemed to delight to take to its bosom. He was the first of that type whom I had met.

Young Dart tutored Kernan for several weeks, and after passing the exam, Kernan invited him to the theater with his father and sister. Dart had "but one suit and was not too well supplied with the other things that gentlefolk wear," but he put himself "in order" and reported to the place where the Kernans were staying. He was on time, but Tom Kernan was not.

> He had all his life the habit of making one wait for him. I started forward toward the middle of the room, tripped on the

carpet and half stumbling, half falling, pulled up beside a bright pretty girl with hazel eyes and a head full of dark curls. It was a laughter stirring plight and she laughed, but as I steadied myself I said my name is Dart and the vision replied, mine is Kernan, and extended her hand and immediately added, you know my father, don't you, and took me over across the room where I was introduced to a tall splendid man, with a head like a God and an eye to comfort and restore any soul, let alone a shy troubled fellow like me.

Shortly after, Tom came in and in due course we were off to the theatre. It is years and years ago, but I never expect to forget that delicious night. There swam into my ken a star of the first magnitude and the star shone on and over me as though I were a planet of equal dignity. It was a night of such absolute happiness that it was never equaled in my life. She was eighteen, slim, trim, erect, buoyant, quick, literate, with a merry silvery laugh.

Two years were to pass before he was to see her or her brother again. Though he was now a full-fledged lawyer with an office of his own, he was still struggling and would never have made the first advances toward people so far above him.

It so happened that on a hot summer day in 1880 he ran into Tom Kernan on the street. Kernan, briefly in New Orleans, was just leaving for Clinton and invited Dart to visit him there, an invitation that was eagerly accepted. He had not seen Mary Kernan since their casual meeting in 1879 but he had never forgotten her. "I proceeded by boat up the Mississippi to Port Hudson, Louisiana, where I took the old and now abandoned train for Clinton, reaching there the afternoon of the second day after my departure."

"At [Tom Kernan's] home I met Mrs. Kernan, his mother. As I came to the door of the parlor she was playing the piano and a little sprite was dancing a jig to this music." Mrs. Kernan "was a cultured woman, a lady in every meaning of the word." The little sprite was Dimple, Mary Kernan's younger sister. Another sister, Darling, was off at school in New Jersey. Then Mary Kernan, who had recently graduated from Silliman Collegiate Institute in Clinton, came in.

I discovered anew the woman who was thereafter for her lifetime to be the ruling feature of my destiny.

She was petite with a quick active movement, small feet, little hands, a mass of brown curls hanging over her back and a bewitching expression. She had and retained to the end the most musical voice I ever heard in woman.

There were dances, wooded walks, horse rides and buggy rides, church service (at which she played the organ) and such other things as you may imagine filled up a glorious ten days. It was August but if it was hot I never discovered it; the nights were full of stars and moon, and we never got to bed until midnight. What a wonder she seemed to me. She had read everything and to end it briefly, I was so madly infatuated on the tenth day as ever I was in the spring of 1878 when she completely filled my boyish vision.

By the time he left for New Orleans they had agreed to correspond. "From one letter we soon advanced to three a week."

Although he was in no position to contemplate marriage, he worked prodigiously toward that end. "I was about as poor in purse as any man who ever sought a lady's favor, but somehow my contact with her had given me a new view on life. I think I always had courage but with her in my mind I became brave." A year later he was able to buy a very small diamond ring, and seven months after that, in April 1882, he says, "I put $75 of my hard earnings into a beautiful pair of bracelets for her, my first serious gift, for the little engagement ring represented only a poor fellow's petty savings."

By late summer he was able to buy a small house on Bordeaux Street between Pitt and Prytania Streets, and on September 27, 1882, two years after he had opened his own law office, they were married quietly in Clinton. The happiest period of his life began.

The bridal couple took a train and boat down the Mississippi River reaching New Orleans the next day. They rode the streetcar to his parents' house where they were greeted with hostility. His family, he says, had led "narrow, unworldly lives" with only one thought, "to fight for a living," so their aversion to Mary, with her aristocratic bearing, was understandable, but "that homecoming was a very unpleasant memory."

They stayed there only one night and moved the next day into their own little house, which they furnished with Mary's trousseau money.

"I had put all the money I had into the purchase of the house. In truth I married with just enough to pay the preacher and our fare home." Her money paid for "a little parlor suite, a bedroom and dining room suite, and I went into debt for the kitchen."

He also went to work with dedication, and he prospered mightily. As his reputation and practice grew, they moved into bigger and grander houses, and within a few years he was affluent enough to buy a summer home on the Mississippi Gulf Coast. A few years after that he built a palatial brick mansion at 5931 St. Charles Avenue, corner of State Street in New Orleans, which was unfortunately demolished some time after World War II.

They had seven children, four boys and three girls, of whom our father, Henry Plauché Dart, Jr., was the eldest. The others were: William Kernan Dart, May W. Dart, John Dart, Benjamin W. Dart, Sally Dart, and Edith Dart (Mrs. H. Grady Price).

As the years went by their way of life became more lavish, and after the turn of the century, it was opulent. Mary Kernan Dart loved parties and the theater, and she loved to entertain. She had china and silverware in matching sets of two and three dozen, and was acknowledged as one of the foremost hostesses in New Orleans. A diary, which is still intact, kept by her second child, William Kernan Dart, tells of balls and cotillions and dinner parties. On Saturday, December 30, 1911, for example, they entertained at dinner before a cotillion. "Thirteen present and we scoffed at the superstition. Mama at her gayest." She was 52 years old, vivacious and never ill. Soon it was all to end.

The first inkling comes a few weeks later on February 15, 1912: "We are all very much worried about Mama," the diary notes. " She cannot keep anything on her stomach." Hardly a day passes without a mention of her.

Henry Plauché Dart

Mary Kernan Dart, the paternal grandmother we never knew

29

Sun. March 17: We called Dr. Cochran in tonight to see Mama. He thinks she may be suffering from gallstones.
Mon. March 18: Cochran further diagnosed Mama today ... it may ultimately result in an operation.

In April she seems to improve.

April 9: Mama is again much better today.
April 14: Mama sits up now about four hours a day.
April 17: Mama seems nervous today, but she is resting easy.
April 18: Dr. Cochran wants to operate on Mama next week. He says it is the only hope.
April 20: Mama seems to be better today.
April 29: Mama does not seem to be well today.
May 7: Mama passed a very poor day.
May 8: Mama is very weak. I am commencing to fear the shadow is hovering too near.
May 9: Bad news today again. Dr. Cochran told me if we failed to operate within two weeks she would die. But the risk of the operation is grave . . . God give us strength to face it if our worst fears are to be realized.

The following days bring excruciating worry to the whole family. The gall bladder operation takes place. There is hope. She improves.

Wed. May 29: Mama consistently improves . . . I suppose she will be in such a condition as to be removed [from the hospital] by Saturday.
Fri. May 31: Mama died this morning at five minutes of seven... God take and protect the best mother man ever had.
Sat. June 1: Oh, Mama, if I only had you back again. If I could only have you around. You forgave a multitude of faults and your trip away has left me stripped by grief. Someday he will call me to you, and then we will be happy forever together. Pray God will take you beneath his shelter. [Bill Dart died six years later in the flu epidemic of 1918.]

The whole family mourned. Her oldest son, Henry (our father), wrote touchingly in his diary on May 31, 1912, "She loved me, I think, a little better than the rest of her children."

Grandpa Dart was devastated. He never got over her death and it may be that he began then to build the protective shell around himself that separated him from us. Our grandmother's death was an incalculable loss for us as well as for him. Over and over people told us of her gaiety and her sense of humor. What an entirely different view we would have had of our Dart heritage had she lived.

After her death Grandpa Dart immersed himself more than ever in his work. In addition to his law practice, he involved himself in civic work. He organized the Louisiana Bar Association and was its president for many years. He became an avid student of Louisiana history, mastering French and Spanish in order to translate early documents. He edited the Louisiana Historical Quarterly for decades. Even in his last illness, he left prepared copy for two issues of the publication.

To say that he went on to the greatest heights is not an exaggeration. The list of his achievements and honors is legendary. He published widely, was an eloquent speaker, a scholarly historian, and above all, one of the most accomplished lawyers in the state of Louisiana.

Another way that the Dart name became well-known, especially among lawyers, was through the series of law books that bore the name Dart. These books for thirty or forty years were the chief source of all the laws in the state of Louisiana with annotations of every case from the inception of the law to the latest case—and brought up to date every year.

The enormous task of annotating all the cases of all the laws in the state was begun in 1912 by Grandpa Dart's second son, William Kernan Dart and was continued by other members of the Dart firm, notably our Uncle Ben Dart, until some time in the 1950s. The books, published by the Bobbs-Merrill Company of Indianapolis, Indiana, were referred to as *Dart's Code of Practice, Dart's Civil Code, Dart's Digest, Dart's Code of Criminal Procedure,* and *Dart's Louisiana Statutes Annotated.* If Louisiana law was involved, these books were essential. Thus the name Dart appeared in every large law library in the country and probably outside the United States as well.

Eventually the task of annotating every new case was so great that outsiders were drafted to assist in the job. Ultimately, a new publisher (the West Publishing Company of St. Paul, Minnesota) took over and hired its own staff. But until then the name Dart was synonymous with the word law in Louisiana.

Years after Grandpa Dart's death, when Harry joined the firm of Dart and Dart, an older lawyer met him and said in tones of awe, "You're Henry Dart's grandson? I knew your grandfather; we had the highest respect for him. He was a real fighter, a man to be feared in the court room."

His reputation is still alive today. To mention a few examples: as recently as 1988, a chair in his honor was established at Louisiana State University, and a collection of his legal papers is in active use at the University of New Orleans. In addition, a bronze bust of him is on display in the Louisiana Supreme Court Building. It stands on a pedestal on the right hand side of the corridor as you enter the court room.

❧

Parents

That the path of our mother, Suzanne Dupaquier, should cross the path of our father, Henry Plauché Dart, Jr., was unlikely. In 1914 she was still living at 819 Orleans Street in the French Quarter, which had long since become unfashionable, while he was living in a fine house uptown. He had been educated at Tulane and Harvard; she had gone to the Sacred Heart Convent and the State Normal School in Nachitoches.

Grand-mère Dupaquier had been easygoing in bringing up her three children. Our mother, born in 1888, was the oldest, followed by St. Marc and Walter. The children, especially the boys, led a more or less carefree life, Notwithstanding their father's erudition, they were not forced to pursue a rigorous educational program. The boys loved the outdoors and often skipped school to go hunting or fishing. Uncle Walter was to become, among other things, a farmer, the role he liked best. He was married to my favorite aunt,

Aunt Alice, and was the father of four wonderful children. Uncle Marc, loved by everyone who knew him, had a series of professions.

Suzanne developed very differently. In spite of her sketchy formal schooling, she became a well-educated person through her own efforts. She was timid around those with a college education, not realizing how superior she was, for unlike most college graduates, who think they are finished when they get their diplomas, she continued to read and learn all her life. The courage it takes to educate oneself is reason enough to be self-assured, but I learned this too late to tell her.

What she did do within the limited framework of her convent education and laissez-faire atmosphere at home, not to mention the pre-World War I attitude toward women, was greatly to her credit. On her own initiative she took herself off to Nachitoches, Louisiana, and in two years had her teaching certificate and a job.

She became a teacher in a one-room school in Bourg, Louisiana, near Houma. She lived with a family named Daspit, who evidently welcomed her warmly because she remained friends with them for years. The pupils in her school were poor. Some, she told me, walked to school barefoot even in winter. She always had the tenderest feelings for poor people and in her unobtrusive way quietly helped them whenever she could. During the depression all of our clothes were carefully mended—even our old shoes were polished and repaired—and given to charity. Later, when she could afford it, her charities were on a larger scale—she was never niggardly. She once paid for the funeral of a servant who had worked for her twenty years earlier.

After teaching for two years, she returned to New Orleans to do something she had always yearned to do, study voice. She sang beautifully and had always loved music, but it apparently had never occurred to her family to offer her music lessons. They didn't even own a piano. So she sang by herself. It was only after she earned her own money in about 1913 that she took herself to Newcomb College music school, which was at that time still on Washington Avenue between Camp and Chestnut Streets. (Newcomb moved uptown near Tulane University in 1918.)

Timid as she was, she met another part-time music student there who

Suzanne Dupaquier before her marriage

befriended her. Sally Dart, daughter of Henry Plauché Dart, who was about her own age, and who was studying the piano, invited the shy young voice student to her home. Never had Suzanne Dupaquier been in such surroundings. After their mother's death, the Dart daughters and their servants maintained the house in the same lavish style as before. It was very different from the quiet shuttered house on Orleans Street with the medical office in the front room. Suzanne Dupaquier was invited to the Darts' home a second time and she accepted.

In addition to their house in New Orleans, the Darts also had their summer home "across the lake" (meaning across Lake Pontchartrain) on the Gulf Coast in Waveland, Mississippi. It was a large rambling house— a place filled with young people, where guests came and went, where

Henry Plauché Dart, Jr. before his marriage

servants did the work, and where parties, picnics, and laughter were the order of the day. She had never seen anything like it.

"Such lavish living," she said when she was telling me how one of the daughters, later to be my Aunt May, one day ordered dinner for twelve people and at last minute told the cook there would be seventeen.

This then was how our mother's path crossed our father's. Their different lifestyles, their different outlooks must have attracted them to each other. He was a promising young lawyer, already a member of the firm that was to flourish as Dart and Dart, and he was strikingly handsome. She was slender and attractive with her uncurled hair and straightforward manner.

They were married on June 9, 1915, but not before Grand-mère and Grand-père had sold the house in the French Quarter and moved uptown to a rented house, 1566 Webster Street, where the wedding took place. Perhaps the French Quarter was not stylish enough for the bride of a Dart,

Suzanne Dupaquier on her wedding day

or perhaps, since that area had already begun to deteriorate, a move was in order. Amusingly enough, the French Quarter, or Vieux Carré, has come around nearly full circle and is becoming a chic place to live.

Although Grand-père went along uncomplainingly with the move, he did not abandon his old patients in what had become distinctly a poor section. He rented an office behind Castaix Pharmacy at Conti and Bourbon Streets, not far from his old house, and took the streetcar down there every day.

The bridal couple rented the house at 6024 Freret Street where Harry was born on May 22, 1917. He was delivered by a stylish obstetrician who did such a bad job that the rest of us were delivered by Grand-père who remained our doctor as long as he lived.

Less than two years after Harry's birth, the Dupaquiers and the young Darts moved to the two houses on South Claiborne and Adams, where the rest of us were born and where we children led such a secure life. If things were tense at our house, we were always welcome next door. Grand-mère rarely left home, and Grand-père rarely came home without a trinket for us. He also brought home exciting packets of colored powders and pills he had received as samples; Ned and I used them with his amused approval as decorations on our mud pies. He was never impatient with us, though five children running through his house must have disturbed him often at his studies.

I remember his reprimanding us only once and then so gently. We had found an old, but still good, straw hat called a straw-katy. We put it at the bottom of the steps in his basement and took turns jumping from a step or two above onto the hat, smashing it to smithereens. Our laughter brought Grand-père from his desk upstairs. He picked up the remains of the hat and said sadly, "Some poor devil could have used this."

We laughed all the louder, saying that if he were a devil he shouldn't have had the hat anyway. Grand-père turned and went quietly up the steps. I knew he was hurt.

He was a person of extraordinary integrity. There is a men's club in New Orleans called the Boston Club which is, I'm told, the *ne plus ultra* of men's clubs with membership into it eagerly sought and zealously held. After my parents' marriage, Grand-père was put up for membership and invited to join, but he declined the invitation, quite possibly the only person ever to have done so. He told his family privately that the club was not democratic enough, but my guess is that he didn't join because it would have bored him to death—also because, like his daughter, he hated pretension of any kind.

This carried over to his profession. He believed that the practice of medicine was a profession of mercy, an awesome responsibility. When he saw how it was being commercialized, how incompetent some of the young doctors were, and how they were puffing themselves up and moving into big offices, he was distressed. Grand-mère told me that some of his white patients left when they saw black people in his waiting room, and that he hadn't even noticed. If kindness is something you learn, we had a living example before us—and also an example of independence. He was a solitary man content with his studies and his family.

We children, on the other hand, seemed to have inherited more of the Dart gregariousness than the Dupaquier timidity—or indifference—whichever it was. And this was one thing wrong with the neighborhood for us. There were not enough children to play with. Although our darling cousins, the five Kernans, the children of our grandmother Dart's much younger brother, lived nearby at 52 Neron Place, we had to cross the canal by a wooden footbridge to get to their house, which we weren't allowed to do alone. Beatrix (whom everyone called "B") and May Kernan were just Ninette's and my ages, and we loved going to their house, especially because their mother, Tante Alice, French like our mother, was just as light-hearted and just as much fun as her daughters. But there were no boys in the family for our brothers to play with, so Harry and Ned had even fewer friends. We certainly didn't have any friends from school.

The year of 1925-26 was a particularly bad one; all of us were home much of the time with one illness after another. Our parents slept in a big four-poster bed in the front bedroom and we slept in five white iron cots in a row on the glassed-in sleeping porch that ran the width of the house overlooking the lawn. If one child caught something, it usually ran through all of us.

That winter Mother nursed four cases of measles, four of chicken pox, and five of whooping cough. The oldest child was eight, the youngest not yet two, and except for Grand-mère and possibly a once-a-week laundress, Mother had no help. She tried to soothe the fierce itching of the chicken pox, but the whooping cough yielded to nothing. I remember the violence of that cough, how uncontrollably our bodies shook, and how the grownups stood by distressed and helpless.

Finally spring came, the illness subsided, and a glorious plan was hatched. All of us—except Grand-père and Dad—would motor north for the summer. Mother would get a rest and we would all avoid the debilitating heat of a New Orleans summer.

Uncle Marc, the older of Mother's two brothers, had married Aunt Mae, a Northerner, and they lived from time to time in New York state, in or near Buffalo. They led a varied life, often traveling around the country by car. Twice they owned and ran a fruit farm. They had no children and would pop in on us unexpectedly in their carefree way, Uncle Marc brimming with fun and tricks for us children. It was undoubtedly he who proposed the trip—one that was to change all our lives, especially Ned's.

He and Aunt Mae had a Model-T Ford and we had a large Studebaker touring car. Mother had not yet learned to drive, so Aunt Mae would drive the Ford and Uncle Marc would follow close behind in the Studebaker.

It was Tuesday, May 18, 1926, a golden, sunshiny day. I remember it perfectly. The two cars were packed and ready in the driveway between the two houses, and we were all happy and excited. After a certain amount of bustle and our last goodbyes to Grand-père and Dad, we took off.

The first day's drive was not memorable. The roads were all gravel and progress was slow. We got no further than Brookhaven, Mississippi, that first day.

The next day, Wednesday, May 19, was again warm and sunny. By early afternoon we were approaching Lexington, Mississippi. I was at the right hand window seat with Grand-mère at my left. Harry, Ninette, and Ned were in our car; Aunt Mae, Mother, and Roger—at the window seat—were ahead in the Ford. We were on a rough narrow road of loose gravel with a deep ditch on the right.

All of a sudden a small truck going pretty fast passed us very close. Everything was partly obscured by the dust, but I saw the truck pass the Ford—very close—and speed on. The Ford swayed. For the longest moment it seemed to hang and sway. Grand-mère saw it too and gripped my hand.

"Pray," she said with an urgency I'd never heard before, and I did. "Our father who art in heaven, hallowed be thy name . . ." I got no further because by then the little car had tumbled like a toy into the ditch. There was confusion. Mother and Aunt Mae were helped out scratched and rumpled but unhurt. It took a long time to extricate Roger. He was still breathing, but he wasn't crying.

My memory jumps next to the hospital waiting room. Mother and Grand-mère were in the operating room where Roger was. Grand-mère came out and said, "Come in and tell your brother goodbye."

There he was lying on his back, on an operating table, his sturdy little legs together and his little brown leather shoes pointing straight up. He had on light blue short pants buttoned to a white shirt which was hardly soiled. He looked asleep with his blond curls tousled, but he made a terrible rattling sound as he took each agonized breath. Mother was at his head and Grand-mère lifted me up to kiss him goodbye. When we went back to the waiting room a young intern was there holding out a brand new package of Wrigley's Spearmint chewing gum and gave us each a piece. He was nice and tried to be playful with us, and I have never forgotten his gesture. Roger died while we each took a stick of gum.

They telephoned Dad who immediately began the sad journey by train to Lexington, Mississippi. We stayed that night in what I think may have been a boarding house. Everyone was exceedingly kind and the next morning, when Ned and I were still in our pajamas (we called them sleepers), a lady told us if we ran outside we'd see her gardener digging up the potatoes we'd have for lunch. Sure enough there was a genial black man digging in the sweetest smelling moist earth I've ever smelled and out came beautiful little new potatoes.

When we came in Grand-mère had a little dress of orange and blue flowers with matching bloomers ready for me to put on, but in all the confusion Ned's clothes and mine got mixed up so that instead of having a pantywaist on which to button my bloomers, she had a pair of Ned's suspenders. I remember setting up a howl, stamping my foot, and refusing to put on anything at all unless she found my pantywaist. She rummaged around in vain, but found a pair of drawers, a one-piece undergarment with a drop seat, that I agreed reluctantly to wear though it meant foregoing the matching bloomers which I loved. I had all too few dresses with matching bloomers because for some reason Mother didn't like them, just as she didn't like underwear with elastic, so we had to wear drawers, which caused us constantly to be unbuttoning buttons— buttons which frequently popped off.

Somehow we made our way back to New Orleans. Thank goodness for Tante Alice Kernan. She was ready to take us away from the gloom. She understood children, and while the funeral was taking place, she took us kids downtown on the streetcar with B and May; the other Kernan girls were much older and didn't come. We had a glorious time. B leaned out of the streetcar window so far she almost fell out, and we all laughed, including Tante Alice, which we thought was the jolliest thing ever. Our parents would not have laughed.

By the time we got back, the funeral was over, but Roger's death was a blow that Mother never got over. How often she was to say, even after we were grown up, that Roger was her most beautiful and brightest child. He was buried in the then new Metairie Cemetery in the Dart plot instead of in the old St. Louis cemetery, where the Dupaquiers were buried.

Every Sunday we went first to Mass at St. Rita's and then out to the cemetery to put flowers on Roger's grave. Mother would kneel and weep over his grave, while we would go off frolicking among the tombs and over the bridges that spanned the man-made streams. A cemetery is a wonderful place for hide and seek.

Maybe we didn't go to the cemetery every Sunday, just as we probably didn't go visit Grandpa Dart every Sunday; it just seemed that we did. But everything was soon to change. Ned had already supplanted Roger as Mother's favorite. And the following summer we moved to a different neighborhood.

❧ EDWARD DART, ARCHITECT

CHAPTER TWO

❧

SCHOOL

In the summer of 1927 we moved to 1803 Jefferson Avenue, corner of Danneel Street, two blocks from St. Charles Avenue. Although we were only a mile and a half from our old neighborhood, everything was so different it was as if we had erased the past and started all over.

Our new house was (and still is) in the same block as the Isidore Newman School, then and now one of New Orleans' best private schools. The house was large and imposing with a front door of polished mahogany and Doric columns on either side. It was painted white and there was a pretty side lawn facing Jefferson Avenue. On the Danneel

1803 Jefferson Avenue in 1927

45

Dart House, 1803 Jefferson Avenue, as it looks today

Street side there was another entrance, almost as impressive as the one in front, and beyond that a backyard with a driveway leading to the garage, which had servants' quarters above. The house, now painted an attractive pinkish beige, is still in good condition. The old garage has been converted into an apartment and a new garage has been built on the lawn facing Jefferson Avenue. A swimming pool has replaced the old driveway and back yard, all of which makes the whole place seem more crowded than in our day. Friends of Ned's, Charles Wesley (Tar Wes) and Anne Ivens Robinson bought the house in 1952. I can remember Anne Ivens as a teenager standing in our front hall and saying how much she liked our house. She and Tar Wes still live there.

The house was not old when we moved in, nor was it a typical New Orleans house. Designed by Richard Churchill, it had been built in about 1910 by Mr. Frank Otis for his mother; upon her death it was sold to a family who sold it to us. Mr. Otis also built the house next door on Jefferson Avenue where he lived alone. That house, along with all the nearby houses on Danneel Street, was demolished in the 1960s to make

Dart House, Danneel Street entrance

way for new buildings for the Newman School. Only 1803 Jefferson Avenue remains.

I do not remember ever seeing or hearing Mr. Otis, so I have no idea how old he was. But he could not have been very old because once when I was ill and lying awake in the middle of a summer's night with the windows open, I heard a woman's voice scream, "Frank, give me back my shoe." That's typical of New Orleans. The houses are close together and neighbors can be as intimate and friendly as one would expect, or they can lead lives closed off from one another.

Mother always claimed she hated "1803," which is what we, and later all of our friends, called the house. She said Dad had closed the deal without her complete acquiescence. Nevertheless from the beginning she lavished care on the furnishings and decoration of the rooms as well as the garden. Even as children we—Ned included—learned to respect her taste, especially in interior design. For the front parlor she bought French antiques and a thick Chinese rug of solid beige with only a muted rose beige border and a single bright blue figure in one corner. Our dining room had two antique marble top sideboards, a mahogany table and fiddle back chairs. Upstairs Ninette and I had matching four-poster beds and walls painted a soft blue. The boys had mahogany spool beds.

The best thing about our new neighborhood was that there were lots of children around. Living in the same block as the Newman School, which we were all ultimately to attend and which became the hub of our lives, we were surrounded by activity. Harry and Ned were enrolled in Newman immediately, but Ninette and I were enrolled in the Sacred Heart Convent on St. Charles Avenue. Mother wanted us to go there because both she and her mother had attended the old Sacred Heart Convent in the French Quarter where French was spoken and good manners stressed. After the convent was moved uptown and the language changed to English, it continued to enjoy its reputation as the finest school for the daughters of aristocratic Catholics.

Sacred Heart Convent, New Orleans

All four of us got completely new outfits for school. Harry and Ned were taken downtown to the boys department of Godchaux's, one of the best stores in town, and Ninette and I got dark navy blue or possibly black, prickly wool skirts, pleated all around, and white starched blouses that scraped the neck. Harry and Ned came home from their first day at school glowing and laughing. Ninette and I came home in tears.

The nuns had not prepared any orientation or greeting for the new girls. Ninette was put in a large class of fourth graders who all knew each other and were standoffish to the newcomer. I was put into a class that had no name and was apparently an afterthought as there was no provision for us whatsoever on that first day. We were deposited in the junior study hall, a dreary room with rows of varnished desks, under the command of an old wizened nun, who simply told us to sit still.

Pretty soon I had to go to the bathroom but was too scared to ask, so I waited in torment. Finally the lunch bell rang and I saw Ninette in the hall where our lunch boxes were kept. In tears I asked her to take me to the toilet. She did, but remember all those buttons on the drop-seated drawers? I didn't make it in time, and the Sacred Heart Convent now had a large puddle on the floor and a crying kid with sopping underpants.

The old nun was furious. She made it clear that I was a disgrace, which I believed, thus adding a load of guilt to the shame and discomfort I was already burdened with. That nun was perhaps not as well suited for handling little children as she might have been. Luckily she called a sweet young nun who took me up flights and flights of stairs to a long dormitory that had two rows of cubicles with a hall running down the center. The cubicles were partitioned off by white cotton curtains on rods. In each cubicle was a cot, a table with a couple of drawers, and a crucifix above the cot. This is where the boarders slept.

The kindly young nun helped me with my wet underwear, which being one piece, involved removing the blouse and the pleated skirt, not to mention one of my socks which was also wet. I waited a long time in that cubicle with only the prickly skirt and starched blouse between me and perdition. My lunch box was still unopened when I got home.

Meanwhile Ned had gone to kindergarten, a word that I had never heard before, a word that sounded bright and beautiful to me. It's a word I still love—so different from Low Primer, which smacks of desks in dim rooms. Mother, who was always careful about words, told us that it meant children's garden and we must never say "kinnergarden" as so many ignorant people did. Ned came home telling about his teacher, Mrs. Anderson, who had, he said, "golden hair." He was mixed up. He meant silver. But she had taught the children songs and shown them how to paint with water-based poster paints on big sheets of white paper set on easels. The children sat in pretty little blue chairs, freshly painted, and had little rag rugs which they used for nap time. Ned loved it. One day he invited a lovely little girl with soft curly hair over to play after school. Mother was with them outside, and she made a wreath of shiny green leaves and twigs which she put on the little girl's head. It was a beautiful picture I never forgot. The little girl was Rita Worms, who still lives in New Orleans and who told me recently, "None of us will ever forget Ned. He was one of my favorite people."

Every morning that year, a much-loved black woman named Liza Lee who lived above the garage(our first full-time servant), walked him to and from kindergarten. I can see them now, hand in hand, going down Danneel Street, he tugging ahead and she, old and heavy, going as fast as she was able. And I can also see Ninette and me, nauseated, as we waited in the kitchen for our lunch boxes and the dreaded trip to the convent. By the end of the year I still could not read.

I do not know whether it was that fact or what, but the following fall all four of us were enrolled in Newman. I was eight and assigned to the third grade. Luckily there were no tests to see if I was ready, as I could never have passed. Nor, luckily, was there any such thing as a learning disability, as I would surely have been branded as learning disabled when all I needed was a proper environment. The Newman School was certainly that.

On that first day in 1928, Ned and I walked together in our new outfits, he so proud to be my guide. We went to the building facing Valmont Street behind the main building and up the big staircase to the third grade room. "This is your room," he said. "If you need me, I'll be downstairs in Miss Nash's first grade room."

Newman School, elementary school entrance (1988 photo). Ned was my guide on my first day.

I can never forget the sheer abundant joy of my first day at Newman. I entered the third grade room with its wide open windows and golden sunlight and the children crowding around to welcome me, the new girl. One blond little girl in a pretty yellow dress, named Jennie Ross, insisted that I sit next to her, and another pushed a green lollipop in my hand and said laughing, "Pass and no pass back." Our teacher had on a light blue dress and was young and pretty. Within a few days I could read.

The happiest days of our lives were just beginning. There were ups and downs, to be sure. Like all kids, when summer vacation came, we chanted "No more pencils, no more books, no more teachers with dirty looks," but we, in fact, loved school and were always happy to go back in the fall.

Newman was not an easy school. Besides the pencils, books, and dirty looks, we had homework, lots of it, and beginning in seventh grade, exams, which we hated. But I cannot remember a single student I disliked nor a teacher who was incompetent or unfit to be with children. I recall instead our eagerness to get to school every day and our reluctance to leave in the afternoon.

In the morning Mr. Mayne, the custodian, or Jason, the janitor, would unlock the doors and let us in, often with a group of us waiting on

Front steps of Newman School

the front steps. I remember especially those soft lyrical days of spring toward the end of the school year when the air was perfumed with the smell of flowers. At that season Augusta Kraak, whose family owned one of the biggest florist operations in town, often had a bunch of sweet smelling gardenias, called cape jasmine in New Orleans, that she divided among us filling the halls and classrooms with their delightful odor. We wore cotton dresses, freshly washed and ironed, and, like most southerners, we observed the ritual of the daily bath. (Later when I went to college in the north I was shocked to discover that many of my peers didn't observe that admirable custom.)

Classes at Newman began at 8:30 and were over at 2:30 with an hour break for lunch. We worked hard, but at 2:30 we were free to leave or to stay in the school playing or working. Many a time, late in the afternoon, I heard Mr. Mayne shooing kids out of the buildings, saying it was way past time to go home, and the kids arguing that they weren't finished whatever it was they were doing.

I remember once working on a project for Latin class to show the English derivatives of the verb *ducere,* to lead. We constructed "the house of *ducere*" with each room representing a derivative ("produce" in the kitchen; "reduce" in the exercise room; "induce" in the children's room, etc.). We complained bitterly about being, as we put it, thrown out before we were done. It amazes me today that children are compelled to stay in school such long hours with such inferior results. I try to figure out exactly what formula—what chemistry—made our school such fun and so superior, and I cannot come up with a simple answer.

Originally called the Isidore Newman Manual Training School, it was founded in 1902 by a Jewish immigrant, Isidore Newman, who had come to New Orleans, steerage class, alone and penniless just before the Civil War. Smart and hard working, he opened his own investment brokerage business after the war and made a fortune. He spent the rest of his life looking for ways to give it away.

His method usually was to stuff a check in an envelope with a note saying, "Enclosed please find check." A few days before Christmas he would take out the city directory and run down the list of charitable institutions in order to send off checks to any he thought deserving. Once he heard that at a Catholic home for orphans, the dormitory for the white children had mosquito bars but the section for the black children did not. When he approached the sister in charge, he was told the reason was not discrimination but lack of funds. He immediately told the sister to order the mosquito bars for the black children and send him the bill.

Newman's concern for orphans is evident in his founding the Newman School. There was an orphanage for Jewish children—and a good one—that had been going since 1855. Newman was one of the directors, and though the children were housed in a substantial brick building on the corner of St. Charles and Jefferson Avenues, he was not satisfied with the kind of education they were receiving. They attended the public schools, which did not have trade school facilities. His concern was that they be self-supporting when they left at age eighteen.

In 1902 he purchased the site for a school that would offer manual training as well as the usual curriculum. It was on Jefferson Avenue between Danneel and Saratoga Streets at the other end of the block in which our house at 1803 Jefferson Avenue was soon to be built. Newman paid $8,000 for the land.

It was assumed that the school would be for the orphans, but before it opened, Newman added a significant provision. A hundred additional students would be admitted regardless of creed or denomination.

In 1904 when the school opened, there were ten paying students. By the end of the school year there were twenty-three, and in no time the number of outsiders had increased far beyond the one hundred Newman had specified. I do not believe anyone, then or ever, counted how many were Jews and how many weren't.

"A good Jew," he once said, "must be a good Christian, and to be a good Christian you must be a good Jew." It was this spirit of bigness that permeated the school, and for that if nothing else all of us who went there are in Newman's debt.

By today's standards we had poor equipment and some rather antiquated teaching methods. We had no counsellors, no remedial reading, no testing—possibly it is just this that made the school what it was. We weren't bogged down with excess baggage. We could simply be what we were: plain teachers and plain students doing the best we could with the things we had. Our school motto was *Discimus Agere Agendo* (we learn to do by doing), not a bad way to learn anything. Harry, Ninette, and I stayed through high school and profited. Ned did not.

Ned was not a success at Newman—not academically, anyway. Socially—yes. Everybody loved him, even the teachers, which proves how forbearing they were—or how winning he was. If there was noise and movement and laughter, Ned was in the thick of it, or more likely the leader. He was a rough, noisy little boy who went tearing through life and tearing through his clothes with the same abandon. When he was still in short pants buttoned to a blouse, the buttons were always popping off usually leaving a large tear in the blouse. Mother and Grand-mère spent hours reinforcing the buttons with neat square patches behind them, only to have the whole shebang break loose at the first wearing. Long after he progressed to regular shirts, his shirttails continued to fly loose. And his

Ned winning a race at the Newman School

voice was formidable. Even his companions, no little angels themselves, often had to tell him to pipe down. In addition to all that, he was an accomplished designer of paper airplanes that went sailing out of school windows during class and paper water bombs that exploded upon impact. The water bombs were reserved for after school when he was "kept in." How often I looked for him after school only to see his face in the window waiting out his punishment. Once or twice I saw him hanging out of the window.

When he wasn't causing trouble or serving time for it, he was busy running and jumping. He was very good at track, earning a certain amount of glory for the school team, especially in the fifty-yard dash. He was very fast—he had had a lot of practice, after all. Needless to say he was never without friends, and living as close to the school as we did, we always had company. Our house was a jolly place. And even though I was two years older, his friends and mine overlapped. This was so all our lives.

Among our first friends after we moved were the children of a large, expansive family nearby. For me, this family epitomizes the flapper era. We had the good fortune to enjoy a couple of years of prosperity before we felt the impact of the great depression of the 1930s, and everyone in this family exuded prosperity. The children, including two or three about our age, lived with their parents and grandmother in a wonderful house with a porch in front and all the doors wide open or at least unlocked.

The older girls, who were in high school or college, were both very pretty and had boyfriends by the dozens. They also had mirrors in their bedrooms so jammed with invitations stuck in the frames that there was hardly any mirror showing. The tops of their dressers were covered with lipsticks and rouge and powder with fluffy down powder puffs. It was the age of the flapper. Parked out front there was always an open roadster, and there were boys in striped blazers and saddle shoes. There were cigarettes, rolled stockings, short skirts, ukuleles, parties and laughter—and maybe even hip flasks.

The constant coming and going was for us an explosion after our quiet and narrow life in the old neighborhood, and we loved it. What impressed us more than anything was that the girls were allowed to go downtown on the streetcar, mostly to the big department store on Canal Street, Maison Blanche, which they called "Maison," and where, to our wide-eyed astonishment, they bought all sorts of things—clothes and cosmetics mostly—which they charged to their grandmother.

As time went on our house, too, became a neighborhood gathering place, especially after we were given three or four puppies as a surprise from Uncle Marc, Mother's brother, who was temporarily visiting friends on a Louisiana sugar plantation. Among the dozens of children attracted by the puppies were Jennie Ross, the little girl who had greeted me so warmly on my first day at Newman; Evelyn Lowe who lived a few doors down Danneel Street; the McClelland twins, Martha and Mary, who lived a block away on Jefferson Avenue; and Ned's good friend, Gus Flaspoller, who lived on the next street over. It was grand until Mother noticed that one of the puppies acted peculiarly and bit Gus on the ear. That dog was put to sleep and its brain tested. We waited anxiously for the report. The dog was rabid. The rest of the puppies were also put down and tested. All were rabid.

Next began the tedious tracking down of every child who had played with the puppies, as any abrasion or cut licked by one of the puppies was cause for alarm. All of us who had even a scratch had to have the Pasteur treatment. The nearer the brain the greater the alarm, so poor Gus Flaspoller had to have twenty-one shots. The rest of us had eleven, one a day in the stomach for eleven days. Every day the amount of the serum was increased, and by the eleventh day the shots had to be administered with huge syringes and were terribly painful. Gus Flaspoller never once complained. He was a courageous little boy. The rest of us were not so brave.

It was about this time that Grand-mère came to live with us. I'm glad she did because otherwise we would have lost touch with our French heritage too soon. Grand-père had died in 1928, not quite a year after we moved. It was a terrible blow for Grand-mère and a loss for all of us, though of course we didn't realize it at the time. I say "of course" because children are so caught up in their own lives that they rarely feel the impact of death or have a place for mourning in their lives. It was only much later when I thought of that sweet, brilliant, humble man that I wept, and then only inwardly.

He had said that he had heart trouble and did not want to exist as an invalid, but I wonder if the real cause of his death was not bereavement, the realization that he had lost us after we moved away. We had raced ahead in our splendid new life in which he had little part. I cannot remember his having been with us once at 1803, and I know he never saw our beautiful pink and blue room upstairs, or met our friends, or decorated a tree for us as he always had done at Christmas time. Nor do I remember going back to the old neighborhood to see him (yet I distinctly remember visits to Grandpa Dart).

Early in the afternoon on March 13, 1928, Grand-père left his office, which was still in the French quarter, saw his last patients, and came home. He entered the house quietly, went to his room, and took out a pistol and shot himself. His beloved Mlle. Eugénie heard the shot. He died in her arms moments later. She was broken hearted.

Grand-mère couldn't take living alone. It was decided that she should come to live with us until she could manage on her own. She stayed about seven years until just before she died. Harry and Ned were put together in one room and Grand-mère installed her big brass double bed and some of her furniture in the vacated bedroom. I think Mother didn't like it too much. For one thing Grand-mère's furnishings jarred with the elegant furnishings of our new house, but we children loved having her there. She was a peace-maker, a believer in treats for children, and a reader of stories like Uncle Wiggily, which she laughed over as much as we did. She had exactly the right idea about how strict one should be with children. Soon after she moved in I had a skin rash which required a stinging ointment. She offered to relieve Mother of the task of applying it, which she did routinely by taking a dab out of the jar with her fingers, and waving it over the rash. She would tell me to howl a little while she laughingly wiped the ointment off her fingers. The jar was thus emptied bit by bit and the rash healed at about the same pace.

Grand-mère had a brother who spent his life traveling and who would always drop in on us between trips. We called him Parrain Felix because he was Mother's godfather (translated his name means Godfather Happy), and he was another bright spot in our lives. Shortly before World War I, at his parents' deaths, he had inherited a modest amount of money. It probably would have been more if his mother had spent less in those fancy shops in Paris, but no matter, it was enough for him to buy a small house in Covington, Louisiana, not far from New Orleans, and to enable him to travel all he wanted. He never married and he never worked a day in his life. He would return to his house in Covington only long enough to unpack his trunks and plan his next trip.

He was a small dapper man, always elegantly dressed and pressed, with grey felt spats, highly polished shoes, a walking stick, and a delicate fragrance of French eau de Cologne. He was the son, don't forget, of the lady who liked French perfumed soaps so much that she went to Paris every year or so to lay in a supply. He would come to us glowing from his latest trip, eager to show off his acquisitions and distribute his gifts, things like costumes from Turkey, heavy with embroidery, and little celluloid eggs that unscrewed to reveal rosaries inside. He had had the rosaries blessed by the Pope and then had laid them on the tomb of Jesus in Jerusalem.

The good fortune that had marked his life also spared him from the great depression. He died in 1929, which was just about the time his money would have run out anyway. Grand-mère had a dignified funeral for him with a casket from Bultman's funeral parlor and burial in the Limongi-Dupaquier tomb in St. Louis cemetery on Esplanade Avenue. The inscriptions on the tomb are still legible.

The crash came a few months later in October and we felt it immediately. Suddenly the world became quiet. The wild flapper era ceased overnight. Skirts that had been short and snappy fell to a decorous middle of the leg—or longer—length. Waists that had been dropped far below the natural waistline were pulled up to where they belonged. The cloche hat, the long beads, the rolled stockings, the striped blazers, ukuleles—all vanished overnight, and all was still. The streets were empty and the world was sober.

The depression hit New Orleans hard, and it is only now, sixty years later, that some of the families we knew will talk about the strategies and petty economies they resorted to in order to survive, things they were shamed into hiding before. For example one prominent family teamed up with a neighboring family and maintained one household between them to save money. They even passed clothes and shoes down the line from one family to the other. It is only recently that they talk about this openly and laugh about it, but it was no laughing matter at the time.

The large, expansive family with whom we had been so friendly moved away from our neighborhood and we lost track of them. Evelyn Lowe left Newman and went to a public school. Others did too. Another unfortunate thing for us was the opening of the Metairie Park Country Day School in the fall of 1929, an inauspicious time for an expensive private school to open. But it, like Newman, managed to keep going and ultimately thrive. In the meanwhile, some of our best friends from Newman transferred there, noticeably reducing the size of our classes.

The depression brought a lot of sadness close to us. A young man we knew lost his job and, desperate to support his wife and their baby, he accepted an offer selling something like vacuum cleaners door to door in a northern city where, hungry, cold and inadequately clothed, he fell sick with a severe ear infection that led to deafness. His wife subsequently divorced him and took their child away. He went to live with his mother in Covington, who rented us her house for the summer of 1934 with the proviso that we hire him to mow the lawn. It was a tragedy to see this strong and handsome young man sweating behind the reel type mower (power mowers were a long way off) for the pittance we paid him. He literally could not hear any sound whatsoever. He never spoke to us. I never saw him smile.

Not all of the depression stories were sad. A family blessed with several beautiful daughters and an aristocratic past—"broken down aristocrats," Mother called them—temporarily moved into a large rented house in a fine neighborhood. The oldest daughter was of debutante age, and though the depression may have dulled the glitter of the Mardi Gras parades and balls, it didn't stop them. Almost daily the picture of the eldest daughter, in an elaborate ball gown and long white kid gloves, could be found in the society pages. In one of the pictures she had three white plumes in her hair like those worn at Buckingham Palace.

Soon after the close of the season she made a grand marriage to someone with money and a bright future, which after all was the point of the whole charade. But, alas, in the meanwhile the youngest sister, dressed rather shabbily, could be seen taking the street car to the public high school a mile or so away, and one day we noticed that she had on two mismatched shoes, one being a gym shoe. But don't grieve. When her time came, she too got the treatment and she too made a grand marriage and she too is nice and rich to this day.

Another story didn't have such a happy ending. The young lady was another impoverished New Orleans beauty, but this one worked hard for a living and for the few luxuries she could afford. She longed for more and finally scraped together enough for a trip to France for shopping and almost certainly for finding a rich husband. Going to Europe, mind you, was so unattainably far from our reach that hardly any of us dared even to dream of it.

Not only did this young lady dream of it, she did it. She did not however, meet her prince charming—not on the trip anyway. She travelled third class and stayed in pensions too modest even for impoverished princes. But she did meet him almost as soon as she got back to New Orleans.

She came back dressed in the most glorious Paris creations New Orleans had ever seen and she looked stunning. I saw her once. She was wearing a pale blue dress with pale blue hat and pale blue kid shoes all exactly matching. I had never seen pale blue shoes before. A handsome young man was helping her into a shiny new maroon colored car. It was just like the ads in glossy magazines.

But sad to say, it was not until after they were married that she discovered the shiny maroon car was all he owned in the world (and even that not fully paid for). He in turn discovered that her luxurious trip was scrimped and scraped for out of a meager salary and not out of the dignified family fortune that he had counted on.

Although our family, like almost every other I knew, had to economize at every turn, we were luckier than many of our friends. The fathers of some of our schoolmates were unemployed and had to scrape to pay the tuition and keep a roof over their heads. In contrast, not only did our father work, but Dart and Dart was one of the leading law firms in the city. We stayed on at 1803, and we always had help.

Liza Lee, who lived above the garage and who had taken Ned to kindergarten, was getting old and longed to go back to her old home in Eufala, Alabama. It was with regret on both sides that we said goodbye. We never saw her again. At just about that time a seventeen-year-old girl named Emma Parker put an ad in the paper, and Mother answered it. Little did we realize what a far-reaching effect this seemingly unimportant turn of events was to have on us.

It is not until you look back on your life that you can measure the influence of certain people or events. None of us, including Emma, I'm sure, knew what an enormous force she exerted with her sweet quiet disposition and her unwavering integrity. Her history is one of courage.

She was born in 1913 in Washington, Louisiana, St. Landry's parish. Her parents, Effie James Parker and Peter Parker, though poor, were able to scratch out a living from the soil and for a while they did all right. They had eight children, seven of whom survived. Emma was the oldest followed by Gladys, Angelina, Melva, Dorothea, Milton, and Benjamin.

When Emma was ten her father died of pneumonia. There was no way her mother could raise seven small children on what she could earn as a field hand—the only work available. So all alone, Effie Parker took her family to New Orleans, where she heard she could get domestic work. She hired out as a servant, found a place where the eight of them could live, sent the children to school, and returned to them every evening. Even after the girls were grown and at work, the family made a point of being together at night.

Emma stayed in school until she was fifteen when she, too, had to go to work. Her first job was with a woman who could not have been particularly kind, for it was then that Emma, hoping for better surroundings, ran the ad that Mother answered. She began working for us in 1930. She did upstairs work while an excellent cook named Stella was in the kitchen. This happy arrangement lasted a few years, probably until about 1933. Ned particularly loved Emma.

"Ned was your mother's favorite," Emma told me long afterward. "She would stand things from him that she wouldn't take from the others. He was always in the ice box and was always kidding around." Emma was right. Mother was a firm disciplinarian and sometimes fiery in her reactions, yet none of us can ever remember her being cross with Ned, who certainly was a pain in the neck at times. Another person Mother never fussed at was Emma, and it's to Emma's credit that this pleasant relationship prevailed—because Mother must have been difficult to work for.

"Oh, yes, she'd get on my back sometimes," Emma said laughingly, "but I knew how to keep the peace." Wise Emma.

Emma Parker Carter (1989 photo)

It is true that Ned could get away with things we wouldn't have dared do. For example Emma told of his saying to her, "Emma, you are going to be our cook." She brushed it off as a childish joke; after all, Stella was the cook.

But Ned had overheard a conversation to the effect that Stella would be leaving for some reason—another departure we all regretted—and that Emma would be asked to take the job as cook. He couldn't wait to tell her. The rest of us would have been punished for interfering, but he was not even called down, and what a cook Emma turned out to be.

She stayed with us fourteen years, and from time to time her sisters worked for us too. When Angelina was still in high school, she came after hours until she could work for us full time. Melva and Gladys also worked for us part-time until they could get full-time jobs. Gladys was later employed by Judge Howard McCaleb's family in Metairie where she stayed until the 1940s, and where her mother also worked. It was by such unremitting hard work that the family stayed together and ultimately prospered. After my family sold 1803 and after World War II was over, I persuaded Emma, by then a widow, to come north to help me out one summer. She stayed on and ultimately got a job at the distinguished Fortnightly Club in Chicago where she worked for the next thirty years. She was so well liked at the Fortnightly that at her thirtieth anniversary, February 1990, they had a celebration for her complete with an orchid corsage and a purse of several thousand dollars.

The lesson the depression taught all of us was how to do a lot with a little. Except in tragic cases like that of the young mother who divorced her husband when his sudden deafness made him unemployable, most families stuck together and found their pleasure in small things.

Some families continued to spend summer vacations in places they'd been going to for years, mostly on the Mississippi Gulf Coast—Waveland, Bay St. Louis, and Pass Christian. Our family went to Clinton, Louisiana, where Grandpa Dart owned a house. He never went there after his wife's death, so he let his children and their families use the house, each for two weeks in the summer. We took as guests our cousins, B and May Kernan and Mary and Albert Dart, the children of Dad's brother, Bill Dart, who had died in the influenza epidemic of 1918. The Kernans' father had died soon after we left the old neighborhood, so it was characteristically thoughtful of Mother to take on four extra children during our two-week vacation. She did it because she hated to see anyone—especially children—denied a pleasure unnecessarily.

Clinton was a quiet place—not a summer resort like the Gulf Coast—which is why Mother liked it so much and wanted to stay longer than two weeks. So for two summers we rented a farm house four miles from town and stayed the whole summer. The house was a plain white frame house amid acres of cotton fields, with only one black sharecropper's family living anywhere near. Because there was nothing to do we children hated it. Except for helping pick cotton, a deadly occupation for a child, and riding on a mule-drawn wagon filled full of cotton to the gin at the end of the summer, I cannot remember a single diversion. Ned and I were so bored that one day after a rain we decided to play pig. Wearing old clothes, we rolled and wallowed in a nice cool mud puddle. We were covered head to foot, laughing and making pig noises until at last we were discovered and scolded, though I suspect that the grownups were secretly amused. It was at a lonely place like the rented farm in Clinton that our need for friends was most keenly felt.

The year 1931 was one of the worst of the depression, yet a way was found for us to take our first real trip away from home since the aborted trip of 1926 when Roger was killed.

Mother, always more alert than Dad about such things, heard about a girls' camp in Abingdon, Virginia, Camp Glenrochie, the oldest girls' camp in America and perhaps in the world. She also learned that a woman in Abingdon named Miss Annie White took visitors and set the best table in Virginia, which certainly proved to be so. Mother lost no time in getting Ninette and me enrolled at the camp; but Miss Annie refused to have young boys stay in her house, so Mother booked herself and the boys in a private home and arranged to eat meals with Miss Annie.

It was an unforgettable experience. We drove up to Virginia in our big old Hupmobile, taking several days for the trip. The roads were poor and motels were unknown, so every night saw us searching in towns like Montgomery, Alabama (the end of our first day's drive) for a tourist home. Tourist homes were private houses with a spare room or two to rent. They advertised themselves by signs outside, and it was usually by the quality of the sign that you could gauge the quality of the house. Many families during the depression made ends meet this way.

As soon as we arrived in Abingdon, Ninette and I, aged thirteen and eleven, were deposited at camp, while Mother and the boys drove off. We had never been away from our family before and were both felled by homesickness, a sickness I had never even heard about. Our cases were so acute that we became physically sick and Mother had to be called in to reassure us.

Every Sunday thereafter, Mother, Harry, and Ned took Ninette and me to Mass at the nearest Catholic Church, in Bristol, Tennessee, and dinner afterwards at Miss Annie's. This always consisted of ham and chicken, several fresh vegetables from the garden, mashed potatoes that were like velvet, hot feather-light rolls, homemade vanilla ice cream and cake. A fine black butler wearing white gloves, served the food and after the meal we would literally lie on the floor groaning with painful pleasure.

During the week Ninette and I, too young and uncritical to complain, were given nourishing but singularly unappetizing food. Aside from that, the camp was lovely and our fellow campers a delight. They were daughters of aristocratic people, mostly Virginians, and I believe all were Episcopalians. Bishop Tucker's daughters were there as was Midge Darst, the daughter of North Carolina's Bishop Darst. We were the only Catholics at the camp which caused raised eyebrows among some of the counselors and teasing questions from the girls. But we got along fine anyhow and to this day have friends we first met at Glenrochie.

The camp was a money-making operation, run by an Englishman we called Pappy Read, who was a teacher at Episcopal High School in Alexandria, Virginia. The equipment was primitive (we slept in tents) and the kitchen facility barely adequate, but we paid so little to go to the camp that he probably had no choice. I remember going into the kitchen after dinner (we took turns clearing the tables) and seeing a little hired girl of thirteen or fourteen washing our plates and glasses (there were about sixty of us) in a single enamel basin full of brown water and dipping them briefly into an equally small and dirty rinsing basin. Today this would horrify me, but we thrived on it.

We sang hymns after supper, a novelty for us as hymn singing was not the custom among Catholics. I came to love the hymns, especially "Now the Day is Over."

At the end of a month, we left for our long postponed motor trip to Buffalo, New York, the trip we had abandoned in 1926. It turned out to be a big bore. We visited Aunt Mae and Uncle Marc Dupaquier, who were living temporarily in a spacious old-fashioned wooden house that had been converted into apartments. Upstairs lived two nice youngish women whose brother, Earl, was a priest. Aside from having lunch with them once or twice and seeing Niagara Falls, there was nothing to do and no children nearby. We suffered there through the whole month of August.

So desperate were Ned and I for some activity that one day we were watering a patch of grass and I was using a cracked milk bottle as a watering pot. The glass broke, slashing off the tip of my middle finger. Though it bled badly, this was the depression and no one considered taking me to a doctor, which probably wouldn't have done any good anyway. The cut healed over a nerve and to this day it hurts if I accidentally strike it against something. What a relief it was to return to New Orleans and our friends and our school.

Ned and I had made a host of friends at school. His most constant companions were Parham Werlein, whose family owned the finest music store in the south, and Billy Patton. If he wasn't at one of their houses after school, they were at ours. The same went for my friends, Jennie Ross, Elisabeth Mason Smith, Augusta Kraak, and any number of others. The house rang with laughter. We built a badminton court on the side lawn— just a net strung between two posts and strings pegged in the ground to mark the boundaries, and more kids than ever flocked to our house.

Ned and Billy Patton, 1930s

For Harry and Ninette it was different. They weren't as gregarious as Ned and I, or perhaps they were less beguiled by the noisy, happy-go-lucky activity we seemed to attract. Harry, brilliant in school, especially in science and math, was the exact opposite of Ned. Both he and Ninette were more serious than we were.

Like most schools in an age when money is essential to their operation, the Newman School today is tireless in trying to keep in touch with the alumni, especially at fiftieth reunion time. Neither Ninette nor Harry went to theirs. Harry marked his by writing the five paragraphs below.

> When I was a skinny kid at Newman School in the dark days of the Great Depression (1931, 1932, 1933, and 1934), the big events in the winter months were the basketball games which were played in the old gym. Believe it or not, students did not get free passes to the games. Student tickets cost 15 cents which was a lot of money in those days. Being on the team was one way to see the games free, but in 1931 I was a freshman in high school, and much too little even to think about going out for the team. And I certainly did not have 15 cents. But when there's a will, there's a way. Albert Terkuhle and I found a tall ladder behind the gym that we propped up to the window immediately behind the scoreboard, which was manned by an upperclassman. We would climb the ladder, and quietly sneak through the window to the platform behind the scoreboard. It would not be long before the scorekeeper discovered us. "What are you doing up here?" he would yell. Whereupon we would jump down to the gym floor and mingle with the crowds. In later years I went out for the team and watched the games from the sidelines.
>
> One of the regular features of the basketball games was Roasty Toasty. Roasty was a shabby looking man who wore a battered brown felt hat and a heavy rumpled brown woolen overcoat that made him look much bigger than he really was. He carried with him a large burlap bag filled with roasted peanuts. Whenever there was a basketball game, Roasty parked himself on the ground near the entrance to the gym with the intention of selling peanuts to those who were going to the game. Roasty was obviously an immigrant for he did not speak more than a few words of English. In general, he could not make himself

understood. I think he came from Greece. Roasty must have been an optimist, for his burlap bag held enough peanuts to supply every fan in the gym with several portions, but unfortunately Roasty did not sell many peanuts. In addition to peanuts, Roasty offered for sale little American flags which he stuck in his hatband, and little rubber gadgets that would make noise when you squeezed them, but nobody bought those things. Money was scarce in those days, and if the boys had money, they would not waste it buying little American flags. That was for dumb immigrants like Roasty. If the boys had a few pennies, they would go down to the Danneel Street Restaurant and Bar where the bartender would sell them cigarettes for one cent each.

The boys teased Roasty a lot. "I will gladly pay you Tuesday for a bag of peanuts today," they would say. Roasty would just mutter something. I always thought it was cruel to tease Roasty. He seemed to be a very nice fellow, and it wasn't his fault that he couldn't speak English.

When Newman played Jesuit High School, the Jesuit students would cruise around Newman School in their Model-A roadsters before the game, singing in loud voices to the tune of The Washington & Lee Swing, "I'm gonna change my name to Finkelstein." They believed apparently that all Newman students were Jewish. That bit of antisemitism irritated me.

In June, 1934, we graduated from Newman, and in September, 1934, most of us went to Tulane. In 1942 most of us went to war, and in 1988, those of us who are left can look back on those days with mixed feelings. There were several faculty members at Newman whom I liked and respected, but none I really loved. There was only one person I felt compassion for. That person was Roasty Toasty.

Harry Dart
Class of '34

I planned a year ahead of time to go to my fiftieth reunion, making sure to see as many old friends as possible. Ned would have, too, if he had made it to graduation. But in spite of his popularity and his energy, his career at Newman went downhill steadily. Some of his teachers were convinced he'd never amount to anything—Mr. Cooksey, the music teacher, in particular.

About the most important event of the school year was the annual operetta held in May. Mr. Cooksey lived for this occasion, training students through the winter for the lead parts, and day after day rehearsing the chorus. The art department designed the costumes and the boys' shop did the scenery. Music and enthusiasm filled the air. As a result the Newman operettas were really very good productions drawing a full house every year.

One year, to everyone's astonishment, Ned landed a small part, probably against Mr. Cooksey's better judgment. Our operettas were generally set in far away, romantic places, where kings and pirates and beautiful damsels played out their parts. Ned was to be a tattered beggar who came on stage briefly to ask the king a favor. His entire role consisted of entering on his knees, stage right, reciting his one line: "A boon, I ask your majesty a boon;" getting kicked; and departing hastily in the direction from which he had entered.

He worked for days on his costume. He got an old Mardi Gras costume which he tore into the most authentic tatters you've ever seen. About noon on the day of the performance, with the encouragement and cooperation of his friends, he rolled in the dirt and put wet mud on his face so that it could be dried and caked by curtain time. It was a lot of trouble for a short appearance, but it turned out to be worthwhile.

When the King said, "Away varlet," and gave him a slight shove with his foot, Ned somehow managed to spiral upward and spin dramatically downward almost into the footlights. He picked himself up amid cheers from his friends, bowed, and made an ostentatious exit stage left. People who can't remember anything about the operetta, even its name, still talk about his brilliant performance and his costume. Mr. Cooksey never let him have another part.

It was soon after that anyhow that Ned left Newman. Perhaps our kind and patient principal, Clarence C. Henson, finally lost patience and suggested Ned's removal, or perhaps Dad saw what was happening. What was clear was that Newman and Ned were on conflicting courses and that something had to be done.

The country was still in the grip of the depression at that time, but things had eased up considerably for our family. In 1933 Ninette and I had been sent to Camp Glenrochie again, and in 1934 Dad had taken Harry and Ned to Chicago to the World's Fair, A Century of Progress, which they never forgot. In the summer of 1936, Harry, who hadn't worked as conscientiously at Tulane as Dad would have liked, was preparing to go to Princeton and Ned and I were both sent to camp.

Ned went to Camp Greenbrier near Alderson, West Virginia, and I went to Camp Sequoia in Bristol, Virginia. I hadn't wanted to go, but like Ned I was underweight and Mother was obsessed with keeping us plump. She heard that the food at Sequoia was good in spite of the astonishingly low fee charged. In fact I don't see how Camp Sequoia managed to give us so much for so little except to say that it was a very well run girls' camp.

It was affiliated with an adjoining women's college called Sullins Junior College where the movie actress Margaret Sullavan had recently been a student. The college had a good reputation, and the camp had good counselors and outstanding food. (I gained thirteen or fourteen more pounds than I needed, which took many years of effort to remove. Mother thought I looked grand—I mean before I lost the excess weight.)

Camp Greenbrier was apparently also a success for Ned as he came home bouncing with good spirits and good health. But even before he returned home, Dad had begun what was to become a voluminous correspondence with J. Carter Walker, headmaster of the Woodberry Forest School in Woodberry Forest, Virginia. In August 1936, Dad sent in the $30 application fee (a large sum in those days) and Mr. Henson sent Ned's transcript along with a letter saying that "young Dart is a splendid boy. You will find him courteous and honest and obedient." But in the interest of prudence, Mr. Henson added, "He is not a brilliant boy, but he will do cheerfully what he is told to do."

In those days children were accustomed to doing cheerfully what they were told to do, and for our part we were just as happy that decisions like where we went to school were made for us. Mother and Dad drove Ned up to Virginia, a grueling three day trip, and they deposited him at Woodberry in time for him to take "qualification tests" on September 23. Then Mother and Dad turned right around for the return trip to New

Orleans. Ned sent them a note saying he had taken the tests and was to be put in form three. On September 29 he wrote his first letter home, which like all his letters in this book, has not been corrected.

Tuesday

Dear Mamma,

How are you and the family? How are Susan and Ninette getting along at school. How is Harry making out at Princeton. I am getting along fine here. I made an 80 on a test in latin yesterday.

We had a football game here between Lane High School of Charlottsville. We won 6-0. After the game Mr. Joe Walker took me riding in his car. Everyone sure is nice here with a few exceptions. All new boys are called rats. All rats cannot talk back to the old boys and my roommate takes advantage of this and is fresh with me all of the time the little Darling comes from Denver Colo. He has a Northern accent. I am about a foot taller than he. I was saying my prayer one night and he made some crack about it. I was mad. I got up and told him a thing or two. And after that he shut up like a clam. I guess I told him.

We went to mass sunday with Miss Hill and had a grand time. I met the pastor there and I also got a pack of envelopes for the sunday collection. We go to early mass next sunday, so I am going to Communion.

Tell Susan that Randolf Scott played golf here a few days ago. I got real close to him. He really is goodlooking. He doesn't look like most of those sissy actors. When I come home I may be good enough to play with Dad. I took a fall track workout yesterday. Mr. Dick is the coach. He sure is nice. I have not been in swimming lately becuse it has gotten to cold. I was in the reading room yesterday, and while looking at the Baltimore Sun I saw that they are going to get some noisless street cars thank goodness. maby the next time we stop there we may sleep in peace. I am sorry that I have not written sooner but you really don't have any time for it. I have gotten a book from the liabrary called wolf. My Wash Cloths have come but my hankerchiefs and grey slacks have not. Congratulate Ninette for me for passing here exam. I received a letter from Susan telling me about Newman. if you see Parham or Billy tell them hello for me Tell Ninette to write.

Your loving son,
Ned

The letter survives intact, along with Mother's heavy black ink corrections. You'll remember that for two years before her marriage she taught grammar school in that small Louisiana town, and she wasn't about to let Ned get away with interrogatory sentences missing their question marks and misspellings like Charlottsville and Randolf and hankerchiefs. As to his erratic and haphazard use of capital letters, she became almost apoplectic. But in the margin next to the part when he tells of the roommate's jeering at his praying, she wrote, "Good for you!!! Bravo!!" She liked a son who said prayers but she was not going to let him get away with a lowercase "m" for Mass. She sent the letter back for him to correct, which he dutifully did.

As the years went by, his letters improved only slightly in orthography and punctuation, and not at all in content. In the four years he was at Woodberry, the gist of his letters was that he was studying tremendously hard, that this test or that exam was incredibly difficult, and that whatever fair, or even sometimes high, mark he got was a triumph. In addition, there was always an account of the latest in sports and games.

His letters have a sycophantic quality. Possibly all children away from home write—or today, say on the telephone—what they think their parents want to hear (my letters from that period have the same buttery tone), but I cringe when I see how scared we were of ruffling Mother's feathers. She was pretty formidable when aroused, unlike Dad who was always gentle, always understanding, always ready to give in.

Most of Ned's letters are addressed to "Dear Mamma" (or Mama). He never wrote to both parents and only a few, mostly about money, were addressed to Dad—Dad who cared so much.

Both parents cared about us, but in such different ways. Dad's way was less obtrusive, more self effacing, and, in the long run, more effective. In the summer of 1937, following Ned's first year at Woodberry, Dad treated the boys to a vacation they forever after considered the best vacation they ever had. He took them out west to a ranch.

It came about partly because Dad had suffered for several summers from a sinus problem for which his doctor recommended the dry air of Arizona. He heard of a working ranch in Bonita, Arizona, called the

76 Ranch (written ⅗) which also took paying guests, or dudes, as they were called. Parham Werlein and Billy Patton were invited to go along to provide the companionship which Ned, in particular, relished.

"The thing I remember best about your family," Parham told me years later, is that your father took us to the ranch that summer of 1937." Parham's father, like Billy Patton's, was dead, and Dad introduced those boys, as well as his own sons, to a wholesome, carefree, outdoor life, that was different from anything they had known before. They came back in robust health and high spirits.

I telephoned Billy Patton, whom I'd not seen for almost fifty years, to ask if he, too, remembered the ranch. Billy became a doctor and moved to Pensacola, Florida, where he still lives.

"Remember the ranch?" he exclaimed. "Of course I do. I can recall that summer better than any other. We had a wonderful time. We rode horses all day, we saw rattlesnakes, and we laughed a lot."

Harry's recollection is also one of rapture: "Dad let us do anything we wanted. It was hot and we'd ride out in the sun, bare to the waist with no hats. It was crazy, as I look back, but it didn't do us any harm. We had BB guns or air rifles and we'd shoot rattlesnakes and jack rabbits. It was good to be free."

While Dad and the boys were at the ranch, Mother drove Ninette and me to North Carolina along with Jennie Ross, from whom I was inseparable, and her mother. A letter from Mother to Ned survives.

Rosscraggon Inn
Skyland, North Carolina
Thursday, July 15, 1937

Dear Ned,

Your letter gave me a great deal of pleasure and I can well imagine how the ranch is ideally suited to Parham's, Billy's and your tastes. Daddy tells me you ride like a cowboy. That is fine, but like anything else be careful. Do not take chances. Be cautious always.

While it is great sport to ride, don't you think you should rest for a part of the day in order to gain some weight? You know you could stand a few more pounds, and that is important to your resistance. Then, too, how about doing some reading? Daddy tells me Mr. Webb has a rather good library. Why not take advantage of it? There is a book I know you would be crazy about and that is "Captains Courageous." See if he has it and start. You'll enjoy it. The picture [i.e. movie] is now showing here in these parts.

Ned, you made a mistake in the meaning of a word which is common, and here is the difference. Your sentence was: "We stood in a log cabin, etc." Stood means standing. What you meant was stayed, which means remained. Son, notice that because you have made that mistake before. No harm meant!! I'm trying to help you. Please learn the difference, won't you?

Now, I want you and Harry to mail a card to each Uncle Marc and Aunt Mae right away. Please tell Harry. Their address is: Barker, New York.

Lunch bell is about to ring so that I must bring my letter to a close with a very sweet kiss. Give my love to Billy and Parham.

Mamma

I'd be willing to bet that he didn't take any rests during the day and I'm positive he didn't read *Captains Courageous* or any other book. He returned to Woodberry no fatter and no more inclined to study. The letters about failed exams, and re-exams, and dropped courses take up where they left off.

How disappointed Dad must have been—Dad, who had himself been such a good student and who dreamed of Ned's going to Princeton. It become clearer and clearer that he'd never make it, and yet Dad never let on that he was disappointed. In fact he cheered Ned on all the more and supported him and set him up again at every downward turn. In March of 1938, his second year at Woodberry, he suffered a downward turn that, if it had not been for Dad, would have been hard to overcome.

He was expelled and sent home with no notice except a telegram from the headmaster saying he was on his way home for having said something unforgivable about one of the teachers. Dad was not told what Ned had said.

Dad, 1930s

Mother, 1930s

It took the better part of two days and a night to go from Virginia to New Orleans in those days, and it cost a considerable sum. When Ned arrived, Dad made him tell exactly what had happened. It turned out that Ned had made a derogatory remark about Mr. John Walker, the headmaster's brother. Either Mr. John, as the boys called him, overheard the remark or it was repeated to him—it had something to do with his lack of prowess on the golf course, if I remember correctly. Whatever it was, it was not very bad, but Dad made Ned sit right down anyhow and write a letter of apology. He then made a reservation for the two of them to return to Woodberry Forest. Dad was at his best when he was smoothing over rough situations. He knew how to handle a damaged ego like Mr. John's, as Ned's letter demonstrates.

Here's Ned's letter shortly after his reinstatement:

April 1, 1938

Dear Mamma,

We arrived all safe and sound Saturday afternoon... After a night at the James Madison [a hotel in Orange, Virginia], to our surprise, Mr. John phoned from Woodberry saying that he would speak with us at the hotel since he had to go to Charlottesville on Business. After a while of talking he came directly to the point, saying the he had decided to accept my apology. Boy, was I relieved. But this is not the end of this incident. After a brief talk with Mr. Carter Walker, Dad told me again, as he had on the trip up, to watch my P's and Q's up here. I certainly agree to what he says, for I think a great deal will count on the manner I act these next sixty days. I am doeing my best to be friendly, kind, and do as well as I can in my work. Also my actions will count. Boisterousness etc. I am doing my best.

His best, at least academically, fell short of success. Letters during his last year at Woodberry (1939-40) were almost exclusively devoted to talk of sports, weekend and vacation plans, his perennial need for money, and his friends. There were by then two other New Orleans boys at Woodberry, Brooke Fox and Charles Wesley (Tar Wes) Robinson. Robinson you'll remember as the one who later bought our house on Jefferson Avenue. Both Robinson and Fox remained friends of Ned's

Patio of the Fox house

until his death, and Fox had Ned design a house for him in 1963 in Gretna, Louisiana. The house is centered around an open patio with a swimming pool in the center.

But that was long after Ned's shaky academic standing at Woodberry. In fact he almost flunked out. A telegram from the headmaster just before Ned was due to graduate broke the news to Dad.

June 5, 1940

Ned has failed to pass English and it is unlikely he will graduate. Everything depends on his passing a re-exam.

Dad's response: "… a keen disappointment since I hoped that he would pass all of his examinations and graduate with honors." Honors indeed. This was typical of Dad's upbeat outlook on life. Mother and Dad cancelled plans for driving up to Virginia for his graduation.

A few days later Ned took the re-exam. His classmates waited outside the building as the teacher graded his paper. The answer came and a cheer went up. They hoisted Ned to their shoulders and carried him off in triumph. He sent a telegram—collect—to Mother and Dad, but it was too late. They could not get to his graduation on time.

Dad was not for one moment angry at the school for the somewhat thoughtless way of handling things. In fact he wrote J. Carter Walker a glowing letter of thanks:

June 22, 1940

Dear Mr. Walker,

This is just a short note to thank you for all that you have done for Ned and to tell you how glad we are to know that he is now an alumnus of Woodberry Forest School. It is also a great satisfaction to know that he has profited so much by his four years at Woodberry. He has developed into a fine manly boy, and we are all very proud of him.

He then requests that Ned's transcripts be sent to the University of Virginia and ends his letter:

I was very sorry indeed that I was unable to attend the graduation exercises. *A combination of circumstances* [italics added] prevented Mrs. Dart and myself from making the trip, but we were nevertheless very happy to know he received his diploma.

With best wishes to you and Mrs. Walker in which Mrs. Dart joins me, I am

Yours Sincerely,
Henry P. Dart, Jr.

Some combination of circumstances. But Ned had passed after all and was admitted to the University of Virginia, which as it turned out was the worst possible place for him to go.

Most New Orleans boys at that time lived at home and went to Tulane University on St. Charles Avenue. Dad had considered it as a possibility,

Ned (ca 1940)

but had written to J. Carter Walker of the danger of a student's being distracted by:

> the social life of the city during the winter months, when the students at Tulane participate to a large extent in the entertainments which are constantly being given. Ned is the type of boy who makes friends easily and would probably be tempted to participate in social affairs here more than he would be, for example, at a college in some small town ... it seems to me that if Ned goes to a college where his work will not be endangered by outside distractions, he would be better off.

At the University of Virginia the outside distractions proved to be the main attraction for Ned. The tone of his letters changes. In his first letter from Charlottesville, he says:

> I love this ole place already ... Sorry I haven't written sooner ... I've met scads of people and feel like I've been here since the days of Thomas Jefferson.
> Tell everyone hello for me and if you see Parham and Billy tell them that I'll write soon—
>
> All love,
> *Neddo*

He was too self-assured. He was snared by, among other things, fraternities. I do not know when we in America are going to graduate from the fraternity system and all of its sophomoric silliness, but it still goes on, helping so few and hurting so many.

In the fall of 1940, Ned was all too willingly swept into the maelstrom of rushing, which was so competitive and so out of control that rules had to be made regulating the times and conditions a fraternity member could court a prospective member. Ned had six "dates" every evening for two weeks and bids from fourteen fraternities. In his next letter home he tells of joining Phi Kappa Sigma which is "tops" and "envied by other fraternities."

Ned's roommate, DeWitt Blundon, who had graduated from

Woodberry with him, wasn't invited to join Phi Kappa Sigma, to Ned's sorrow because "he doesn't make such a good first impression—and that is essential in this type of rushing." Such was the shallow basis for choosing members. It was not until the following year that Blundon, at Ned's insistence, was taken in.

In the meanwhile Ned's first year at the University was such a complexity of social commitments that it was all he could do to keep his engagements from conflicting with one another. As early as November he writes: "Dearest Mother." ("Mamma" is behind him.)

> No, I did not get to see very much of Dad during his stay here. Really I'm very sorry, but you see he came at the wrong time. That week-end, everyone had dates and the dances were in full swing ... Truly, I'm sorry for I'd have loved to spend the whole time with him. Please make it clear to Dad that I, by no means, meant to leave him Saturday afternoon after the game but you know how it is with a date.

A few sentences later he says:

> Oh Mother, when you mentioned that I should buy tails I really felt like a heel after the way I've neglected you and Dad. You're always sweet to me and when I do things like failing to write or do poorly in my work, I feel about as high as an ant. You know how I love clothes and I'd like some tails. If you really think I should have them I'll look around. If possible I'm going to get a coat to match my tux pants. Just leave it to me—I'll do my best to get everything fixed. I'll keep the price under $35.00 too. But as for white gloves, I'm afraid I couldn't bear to wear them. I know it's the correct thing to do, but it looks so awfully effeminate. Couldn't you picture me in white gloves—oh Mother we'll have to settle that point when we get home.
>
> Well sugar plum, I surely appreciate all you're doing for me and thanx loads. I've got to go now—Please write soon—
>
> All my love,
> *Neddo*

Studies are rarely mentioned, but he did engage in one or two worthwhile endeavors. One was sports. In spite of smoking, drinking and partying, he was able to keep in good physical condition, working out at track and other sports.

Another successful endeavor was to sign up in October, 1940, for the Naval Reserve Officers' Training Corps (ROTC) unit that had just been started at the university. To join he needed Dad's permission which was readily granted. He apparently took it seriously.

By the end of the school year, June 1941, Ned was 19 and wanted to join the service full-time. The war in Europe had escalated and possible United States involvement was on everyone's mind. Again he needed Dad's permission and this time Dad refused. Ned's grades had come through and Dad's reason was that Ned would in that case leave the University with the unenviable, and possibly unmatched, record of four Fs and a D (and I'm not too sure of the D).

The rest of us meanwhile had done well. Harry had graduated from Princeton and was studying law at the University of Michigan. Ninette had graduated from Newcomb College in New Orleans where she majored in French, and I was completing my junior year at Connecticut College in New London.

Ned was the only academic failure. But Dad was firm. He told him he had to go back and repeat—and pass—the subjects he had failed. "Leave with a clean slate," Dad said.

He also got Ned a summer job. It was working with the surveying team of a company laying a gas pipeline in Mississippi. It was a tough job and Ned succeeded. He was well-liked by his bosses and fellow workers and worked like a professional under conditions that by today's air-conditioned standards must have been inhumane. He slashed through swamps knee-deep in mud, and toiled for hours in corn fields in the blazing sun. He was paid $125 a month (an excellent salary then) with room at a local hotel paid by the company. His letters are written on stationery from old-fashioned hotels like the McColgan in McComb, Mississippi, whose motto was, "It's homelike," and the Hotel Pinehurst in Laurel. Hotels like these were big and imposing-looking, with potted palms and easy chairs in the front lobbies. But upstairs the rooms were beginning to take on the shabby look that helped put them out of business when clean new motels sprang up after World War II.

While Ned was working in Mississippi, Ninette and I spent a month or so in Wisconsin at St. John's Military Academy, which rented rooms to summer visitors who were allowed to use the athletic facilities of the two summer camps owned by the school. It was a glorious summer of outdoor fun for both of us. At the end of the summer Mother and Dad drove up to get us, and on the way home we stopped to see Ned in Laurel, Mississippi. He looked tan and fit. He liked the job and had done well.

But when he returned to the University of Virginia that fall, he resumed his reckless, dissipated life. He was invited to join one of the oldest and most exclusive drinking clubs on campus, Eli Banana—as if students like Ned, or indeed students anywhere, ever needed such a society. What is astonishing is that he managed to pass (just barely) the subjects he carried—probably the same ones he had flunked the year before—and even do well in ROTC.

ROTC was the only thing he took seriously. There he came to know a senior named Clinton Harbison, who was to play an enormous part, albeit unwittingly, in Ned's 180 degree change from playboy to what he would become. Like Ned, Harbison was lighthearted and carefree, but unlike Ned, he was a good student and responsible.

He came from a prominent southern family; had graduated from Episcopal High School in Alexandria, Virginia; and four years later graduated with ease from the University of Virginia. He had already joined the Navy in January, 1942, less than a month after Pearl Harbor, but was given leave to stay at the University until June to get his degree.

After Dad saw Ned's grades he gave his permission for him to join too. But by then Ned was twenty, the war was in full swing, and nobody could have kept him back. He enlisted at the end of his second freshman year, on June 9, 1942. I had not seen him since Christmas vacation and would not see him again until May, 1943. That year and a half would bring enormous changes in all of our lives—especially Ned's.

CHAPTER THREE

❧

WAR

It was incredible—it is still incredible— how fast things moved as soon as the United States entered the war. Everything changed overnight. The mood, like the mood at the beginning of most wars, was one of excitement and eagerness—eagerness to get on with it. There was an air everywhere of youth and vigor and—yes— happiness. The only really unhappy people I knew were the 4-Fs.

We learned early the military jargon. The army's classification of 1-A meant that a young man was top Army material, physically and emotionally. Four-F meant he wasn't. A song that went something like "He's 1-A in the Army and he's A-1 in my heart," became popular immediately. One pert young girl altered the words to fit her dilemma, "He's 1-A in the army, but he's 4-F in my heart." Romances bloomed and wilted with the speed of light.

Another term we picked up was GI, which stood for government issue but which came to be used as a noun as well as an adjective. Thus a soldier in a GI uniform became himself a GI.

Incidentally the terms girl and boy were universally used for people under about 30 or 35. We would have scoffed at the idea of calling ourselves men and women. It was "our boys overseas," the "girl he left behind," etc. I can't recall exactly when the change came about except to say it was well after World War II.

Perhaps the biggest effect on our lives after Pearl Harbor was in our mobility. I knew hardly anyone my age who didn't go somewhere away from home during the four years we were at war. As a result, travel became difficult. Commercial air travel was still so new and expensive that it was

Ned, 1943

all but out of the question, and anyway a plane reservation was next to impossible for a civilian to obtain. If by some miracle you did get one, you stood a good chance of being bumped. The military had priority.

Gasoline was rationed, so travel by car was rarely feasible for short trips and never for long ones. We went by train or by bus, conditions were always unpredictable, and we were challenged by the ubiquitous reminder, "Is this trip necessary?"

Even long distance telephone calls were so expensive that we didn't make them except in extreme emergencies. Ned and I didn't see each other or talk to each other from Christmas 1941, when we were both home from college, to May 1943, when he came home for his first brief leave.

I was already married by then, but neither he nor Harry, who was in the Army, had even asked for leave to come to my wedding. It would have been denied had they been so brash as to try.

When Ned completed Naval ROTC at the University of Virginia in 1942, he applied for Naval Aviation and when he got his first assignment, he and Clinton Harbison were overjoyed to find that they would be together. On June 25 they reported for duty in Athens, Georgia, where they would face their first hurdle, pre-flight training. And like many others in all branches of the service, they were to acquire nicknames, which in their cases lasted the rest of their lives. Clinton was called Bobo, a name he may have acquired earlier at the University, and Ned was called Ed or Eddie. Although he was never again called Ned except by those who knew him before the war, I shall continue to refer to him as Ned except when some other designation is clearly called for.

Pre-flight training was a three-month stint of hard physical training and demanding classroom work. Half of the day was devoted to exercise, marching, and drill, and the other half to classes in subjects such as math and plane recognition. Some of the men were screened out during this first phase. Dart and Harbison passed easily, which is the first time Ned passed any classroom subject without a struggle. Another candidate who passed easily was Bill Senhauser, a graduate of Duke University from Zanesville, Ohio. He became the third member of an inseparable trio.

Things began to move fast for those who made it. They went immediately from pre-flight to primary flight training. Dart, Harbison, and Senhauser were assigned to Anacostia, in the District of Columbia across the Potomac from National Airport. The training was intense. After only eight hours of flying with an instructor, they were required to solo. Some weren't ready and washed out. Ned passed with flying colors. He had always loved planes, and this, his first experience in the air, was exhilarating. He even copied a few lines from a poem, which was uncharacteristic of him, poetry not being something he read much of.

> Oh, I have slipped the surly bonds of earth
> And danced the skies on laughter-silvered wings;
> Sunward I've climbed and joined the tumbling mirth
> Of sun-split clouds and done a hundred things
> You have not dreamed of . . .

The poem, called "High Flight," had been written by a nineteen-year old who was killed in training in 1941 (see Appendix).

For those who soloed successfully, the training became even more intense. They flew small biplanes, painted yellow, which they dubbed "yellow perils" and in which they practiced formation flying and aerobatics, loops, snaprolls, and other maneuvers. They had to complete 90 hours of flying before they could go on to the next phase of their training.

Many had fallen by the wayside during their three months at Anacostia, but Dart, Harbison, and Senhauser were on the list of those chosen to go on—and all three were ordered to report to the Naval Air Station in Pensacola, Florida, for intermediate training. They were never to be separated until the end.

At Pensacola the training became even stiffer. They were there from December, 1942, to May, 1943, flying low wing monoplanes. The original three were joined by two or three others, who it turned out would also stick with them until the end. Elmer ("Elm") Filkins from Massachusetts and Rodney Marshall ("Rod") Coggin from Virginia were two of that group, and we are still in touch with them.

In the same training group Ned also saw Howard McCaleb from New Orleans. Though about the same age, they had known each other only slightly because they had gone to different schools. Howard had gone to Country Day, but coincidentally their cook, Effie Parker, was our beloved Emma's mother—that brave woman who had travelled with her seven children from up country Louisiana to New Orleans to get a job that paid enough to support her family. She continued to work for the McCalebs almost until her death.

Howard McCaleb, who still lives in New Orleans, remembers Ned at Pensacola. "God, he was good-looking—small but with a beautiful build. He was very athletic—he'd do hand stands—and he had a big influence on the other fellows. He was the sort of guy that other people admired." McCaleb was to be sent from Pensacola to the New Hebrides Islands and consequently lost track of Ned.

Toward the end of their stint in Pensacola there was the choice of staying in the Navy or joining the Marines. Harbison, Senhauser, Coggin, Filkins, and Ned all chose the Marines. "The only difference then," says Filkins, "is that we switched from black ties to khaki." They would later get complete Marine uniforms and develop the pride characteristic of the Marines. In the meanwhile they faced another choice: dive bombers or fighters. They chose dive bombers.

In May 1943, they got their wings, their commissions as second lieutenants in the Marine Corps, and their orders to report to Cecil Field in Jacksonville, Florida, for dive bomber training. They had four days to get there.

Ned in dive bomber

This was the longest free time they had had since joining the service, and they didn't waste a minute. Ned invited Harbison, Senhauser, and a couple of others to come to New Orleans. Senhauser and his fiancee, Wilma Plansoen, who had come down from Nutley, New Jersey, stayed in two different hotels—not even in different rooms in the same hotel— an example of how times have changed. Ned, Bobo Harbison and, I believe, one other stayed at 1803 Jefferson Avenue, where there was room because Ninette was the only one of us children still living at home.

Harry had joined the Army and was away at officers' training school. I was married and living in an apartment on St. Charles Avenue with my husband, John McCutcheon, whom I had married early in 1943 after having known him for only seven months, six weeks of which was engagement. He was called Jack by his friends and was a lieutenant, junior grade, in the Navy. A Chicagoan and a graduate of Harvard, he had been called to active duty in the Navy before Pearl Harbor and was assigned to the Naval Reserve Aviation Base in New Orleans.

Our meeting and marriage was another example of how the war accelerated things. My sister, who had met him earlier, introduced us in July, by October we were unofficially engaged, and in December our wedding date was set. An engagement of six weeks was considered long in those days. I know of couples who met, married, and were separated (by military orders, not choice) within the span of a week. As far as I know all these marriages proved successful. Compare them to the couples today who live together for years before marriage only to fight like dogs after they become man and wife and wind up in the divorce court.

In the spring of 1943, while Harry and Ned were in training and Jack was preparing to go overseas, Ninette was working in one of the many wartime jobs that had opened up in New Orleans. Hers was top secret. She could never tell us where she worked or what she did until after the war was over. It turned out she had been in censorship as a French and Spanish translator.

Ned and his friends came to New Orleans to celebrate their gradua- tion, and New Orleans was certainly the place to do that. I saw them only fleetingly, but every moment I was with them is etched in my memory. We knew even at the time that certain things—especially meetings with people you loved—had to be remembered. I remember Bobo Harbison and Ned laughing and joking together. They were on the porch at 1803 which Mother had enlarged so that it ran across the entire back of the house, continuing the terra cotta tile floor of the original porch. The porch was arranged as a cool outdoor living room with an overhead fan and white wicker furniture with cushions covered in a brilliant blue flowered chintz. It was one of the nicest porches I've ever seen. Mother was the first person I knew who used white and bright blue so daringly. Most rooms at that time—porches especially—were decorated in more practical and somber colors—green mostly. Ours was bright and inviting.

Ned's friends were all handsome. Was there ever anything more splendid than all those fine young men in their immaculate white dress uniforms going off to war? We had no idea what was to come, and I can't help thinking now of that World War I poem called "Disabled" by Wilfred Owen:

> He sat in a wheeled chair, waiting for dark,
> And shivered in his ghastly suit of grey,
> Legless, sewn short at elbow ...
> Someone had said he'd look a good in kilts,
> That's why ...
> He asked to join.

Wilfred Owen was killed in action soon after he wrote that. He was twenty-five.

But in 1943, a mere twenty-five years after Owen's poem and the end of the bloody horror of World War I, we still hadn't learned how cruel this war was to be for us. We were all in high spirits. Ned's was a rowdy bunch having a fine time and eager to get on with the next step. There was noise and wholesome merriment. Going off to war was not like going back to school. It was exciting.

Bill Senhauser and Wilma Plansoen were quieter than the others. I remember her as the slenderest slip of a girl, pretty and soft-voiced. I saw her once or twice and can even remember the white cotton blouse she wore and the simple cotton skirt. In a few days they were gone. The men were off to Jacksonville and Wilma took the train back home to New Jersey. Everything was quiet again.

At Cecil Field in Jacksonville dive bomber training began. They learned to fly at 10,000 feet, drop to 1,000 feet, and make a U-turn upward again. Blacking out—or losing consciousness—was a recurring problem for some, but they pressed on.

Six weeks later, in July 1943, they were in Glenview, Illinois for a week of carrier landing training. Two carriers (actually they were excursion boats sheared off to resemble carriers), the USS Wolverine and the USS Sable, were anchored in Lake Michigan, and by the end of the war 15,000 pilots had each spent a week practicing on them. A pilot had to take off and land eight times during the week's training—and he couldn't waste any time because the planes landed at ten-second intervals. When his turn came he had to act fast. Many failed. As late as 1990, two Navy planes were hauled up from the lake with estimates of as many as 200 more military aircraft still at the bottom. Some pilots escaped with their lives. Some didn't.

By the middle of July the training was over for Ned and his friends. In one year and twelve days they had gone from complete novices to experienced flyers. And they were good.

They got a two-week leave before shipping out, and Ned came home, but I missed seeing him. I was in Lake Forest, Illinois, visiting my parents-in-law. On July 30, 1943 he left for San Diego.

That same day Dad wrote a letter to Woodberry Forest in answer to a question about Ned's military activities from Mrs. Raleigh Taylor, who was in charge of alumni news. Dad's letter to her shows how proud he was of Ned's record—about time too for poor Dad to get some reward for all his efforts.

New Orleans
July 30, 1943

Dear Mrs. Taylor:

I received your kind letter of July 19th and thank you for sending us the 1943 Alumni Bulletin. I gave it to Ned who has been with us at home for two weeks. He was very much interested in reading the news of the alumni and particularly of his classmates.

As you probably know, he enlisted in Naval Aviation in June, 1942, after finishing his Sophomore Year at the University in good standing, and went to Athens, Ga., for preflight training. After that, he was transferred to Anacostia and then to Pensacola, where in May, 1943, he was commissioned a second lieutenant in the Marines. Since then he has been to Jacksonville and Chicago and leaves tonight for San Diego. He looks fine and is very happy and enthusiastic about his work.

I do not know Ned's San Diego address but no doubt he will write you as soon as he gets located. He enjoyed your letter and the Bulletin and says that he hopes you will continue to send the Bulletin to him.

We were of course very glad to have Ned with us, even for such a short time and hate to see him go. On the other hand he would be very unhappy if he had to stay home. I know that you and Mr. Taylor feel the same way about your son and that you are also proud of the fine record he is making. Let us hope that this old war will be over soon.

Sincerely Yours,
Henry P. Dart, Jr.

The eagerness to go overseas was almost universal. The disappointment of those left behind became in many cases a cause for shame. Of the dozen or so men of that age group who, for one reason or another, didn't go overseas, only one took the matter lightly—and maybe even he (deferred because he was a school teacher) was putting on a good front. I know a couple of men, 4-Fs, who to this day are uneasy when World War II is discussed in their presence.

In San Diego assignments were made, and Ned and his group found themselves in a large pool of dive bomber and fighter pilots headed for the Pacific. They were all put on a Marine attack ship and deposited on American Samoa. They were glad that they were still together but knew their chances of staying so were slim. The Marine Corps was not in the habit of asking people who their favorite buddies were.

May, 1944 (l. to r.) Bill Senhauser, Ned, T. Waller, and J.J. Hultgren

Sure enough, in Samoa the assignment to squadrons was made apparently on alphabetical lines. Thus all of Ned's friends, except one, were together: Coggin, Dart, Filkins, Harbison, J. J. Hultgren, whom they got to know in Samoa, and a couple of others. But Senhauser, at the other end of the alphabet, was out. He wanted so much to be with the group that he scurried around and found someone willing to trade with him. At the last moment he was switched over. The gang would go on together after all.

Very soon there was a call for volunteers for Wallis Island. None of the group had heard of Wallis Island, but Ned said it sounded good, so he volunteered. The others did too.

"He was the kind of person you wanted to be with," Rod Coggin told me recently. "We wanted to go where he wanted to go."

Wallis Island is a small dot on the map about 250 miles west of the

Samoan Islands in Polynesia. It was not one of the islands that figured dramatically in the war, being too far away from the battle zones. In fact, it served only as a jumping off place for American airmen, and few of us at home even heard of it until after the war was over.

The men overseas were never allowed to tell where they were stationed. Their families knew only that they were in the Pacific or the ETO, as the European Theater of Operations was called, and that much we knew only from the address we were given: care of the military post office in San Francisco or New York. After our letters left San Francisco or New York we had no idea where they'd end up, and we began to think the authorities didn't either. It took weeks, sometimes months, for letters to get through. But Wallis Island, remote as it was, was no worse than Hawaii, where Harry was, or a ship in the Pacific where my husband was.

Wallis Island, or Uvea, as it is called by the natives, never was in the forefront of history. It was discovered in 1767 by the British explorer, Samuel Wallis, who had discovered Tahiti, and who hadn't even bothered to come ashore on the island later named after him. Except for naming it, the British made no impact there whatsoever. Seventy years later, in

Wallis Island (Philippe Godard photo)

1837, a French Marist missionary established a mission there, and it has been a possession of France ever since. It became a protectorate in 1842, a colony in 1913, and is today a French Overseas Territory.

Like most Pacific Islands, Wallis does not stand alone. It is in a group with two other islands, Futuna and Alofi, and about twenty small uninhabited islets, most of which are mere jutting rocks. But since Futuna is 112 miles away from Wallis and Alofi even farther, the Americans who arrived on Wallis saw nothing but the sea around them.

The island is small—only twenty-three square miles—and the climate is hot and humid. There is no natural recreation—no bathing beaches, scenic waterfalls, or mountain trails. It is surrounded by an almost solid barrier reef broken in only one place wide enough for a ship to pass through. The lagoon is shallow with jagged coral rocks near the surface—no good for swimming.

As for the native Polynesians, the Marines saw them only from a distance. As at most of the wartime island bases, there was almost no contact between the natives and military personnel. If there was a situation anywhere in the Pacific even remotely like the one in *South Pacific* with Bloody Mary chewing betel nut, a romance with a beautiful maiden, and Bali Ha'i in the distance, I never heard of it.

Ned and his squadron of twenty men arrived on Wallis on August 26, 1943. They were housed in small Quonset huts, four men to a hut. Harbison, Senhauser, and one other, were in a hut with Dart; Coggin, Filkins, and Hultgren were in the next hut with a man named Griffin.

Their military duty on Wallis wasn't strenuous. It consisted mostly of flying out on patrols looking for Japanese planes and ships. A brief explanation of what was going on in the Pacific may help to understand the Allied strategy.

After World War I, the Japanese had been given a mandate over a string of islands in the Pacific reaching from the Marianas (except Guam which the United States had had since the end of the Spanish-American War) through the Carolines to the Marshalls. The mandate was designed to promote the welfare of the natives on those islands, which was the last thing Japan had a mind to do.

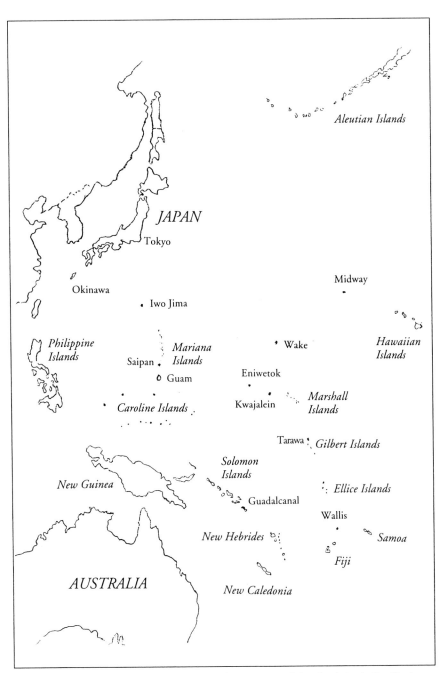

Map showing some of the islands in the Pacific theater

What Japan really wanted was resources—especially oil and metal—to promote her economy. Long before the war started in Europe in 1939, Japan had begun expanding her empire by conquering Manchuria and parts of China, and gaining control of the coast of French Indo-China. But Japan wanted more than that. She wanted domination over all of China and also the Dutch East Indies with their rich resources.

Japan saw no way to get what she wanted short of war. By December 7, 1941, she was well prepared. In one hour she smashed the United States fleet at Pearl harbor (2,403 dead; 1,178 wounded) which in effect eliminated all opposition to her domination of the entire Pacific—at least for the time being.

The next day the attack on the Philippines began, and though we held out for five months, it was a hopeless situation. Japan was clearly in control.

On December 10, 1941, Guam fell (not to be recaptured until 1944), followed in quick succession by Wake Island, Hong Kong, Singapore, Burma, and Borneo. By the middle of 1942 Japan controlled everything—everything but the will of the American people—that could possibly stand in her way to get what she wanted—dominion over the entire Pacific area. She thought the war would be over in a matter of days.

It was the darkest period of the war for us, but we struggled on with a degree of courage and determination the Japanese could not have anticipated. We also had a strategy—a strategy that would ultimately turn the tide.

There was no way we could retake every Japanese-held island. Instead the plan was to attack and seize an island, leapfrog over countless other Japanese-held islands, seize another island, and so on toward Japan. The leap-frogged bases were thus cut off from their supply lines and rendered impotent. But it was a long hard fight because the Japanese strategy was to fight to the last man and never surrender. Thus the fight would have to go on until Japan itself was invaded.

Back at home we followed the news as we had never followed it before. Names we had never heard of—Wake, Bataan, Corregidor, Guadalcanal—became familiar, and terms we hadn't known—archipelago, atoll—

Ned and an unidentified friend

became part of our vocabularies.

In August 1943, when Ned and his friends arrived at Wallis, they were still a carefree bunch. "Eddie," Coggin says "was as usual the leader of any activity that was fun." He tells of Ned's invention of an automatic washing machine of dubious efficiency made from a discarded motor and propeller. "He called it a Fofo machine and he never minded how much we laughed at him." Coggin, Filkins, and Hultgren, who supplied much of the wartime information about Ned, all mention poker as their chief pastime. "We had a limit of $300," Filkins says, "and once I was losing and Eddie said to me, 'Elm, I'll give you all you want.' He was that type of guy—generous. If we went anyplace, we always wanted Eddie to come along. He could have been anything he wanted."

On Wallis they would fly out in pairs—two planes at a time, the lead man and his gunner and the wing man and his gunner. Though they made light of it, and still do, there was a certain amount of risk involved. Losing consciousness was still a common problem, and even if a pilot didn't black out, "water looks the same at 10,000 feet as it does at 1,000," Hultgren told me. Accidents happened.

Griffin was the first man in the squadron to lose his life. A divinity student in civilian life and quieter than the others, he nevertheless loved the excitement of flying as much as they did. "If I get killed flying," he told Filkins one night, "I'll die happy." His plane was shot down and lost the next day. He had been on duty in the Pacific two weeks.

Harbison's number came up next. On September 20, 1943, only twenty-six days after they were "in the field" as the Marine Corps' Abstract of Service expresses it, he was sent out as wing man on a routine patrol mission—four men in two planes—200 miles out and 200 miles back. They did not see any Japanese planes. When the lead man returned, Harbison was not with him. His plane had simply disappeared. Search parties were sent out immediately, but there was no trace. For a while they held out hope and he was listed as missing.

Ten days after his disappearance, Harbison's parents in Lexington, Kentucky, received a telegram from the Marine Corps. That night Mother received a person-to-person long distance call. It was from Lexington, Kentucky. In those days an operator came on and announced the call, and lines crackled. It was Mrs. Harbison. She first apologized for calling Mother without having been formally introduced. She was gentle and polite, even in her distress. She explained that she could not help herself. She was grasping for any thread of hope. She asked Mother if she had heard anything from Ned about her son. When Mother said she had heard nothing from Ned, Mrs. Harbison broke down and wept.

Eleven days later, October 11, 1943, Mr. and Mrs. Harbison received another telegram from the Marine Corps. Their son was officially dead. Mrs. Harbison wanted to let Mother know immediately so she sent a telegram. Telegrams, which had formerly been delivered in yellow envelopes by Western Union boys on bicycles had just begun to be telephoned in as a wartime expedient.

Mother, who never forgot the little son she had lost, called Mrs. Harbison at once. All Mother said after she hung up was, "Bobo was their only child." She was so shattered, she had to leave the room. We heard her weeping behind her closed door.

The next day, October 12, 1943, the Lexington newspaper ran Harbison's obituary with his picture, and the next month the University

Clinton (Bobo) Harbison, killed September 20, 1943

of Virginia's alumni news came out with the news. Under its regular wartime feature called "Their Victory Won," it listed alumni killed in action.

Upon receiving a copy, Major Harbison wrote to the editor.

Lexington, Ky.
18 November 1943

Dear Sir:

I thank you for sending me the copy of your November issue containing on page 14, the listing of my son, 2nd Lieut. Clinton M. Harbison, USMCR, as missing in action.

It is true that the first report was that he was missing: the official telegram, received September 30th, said he was missing after an airplane crash at sea. But later, on October 11, the second telegram said that he had been killed in the crash ...

A memorial service was held for our son and his rear gunner in their unit in the South Pacific on the 6th of October; and at that service, in addition to the regular religious features, there was read the poem "A Comrade Rides Ahead," by Douglas Malloch ... Not knowing that that service had been held, our Bishop here held another memorial Service in honor of our son, in Christ Church, Lexington, on October 16th ...

I like the heading you give to the column in which you list those lost in service in the armed forces, "Their Victory Won." I assume it comes from the beautiful old hymn.

"The strife is o'er, the battle won,
The victory of life is won;
The song of triumph has begun."

The letter ends with a heartbreakingly courageous paragraph from the father of an only son:

I have read the Bulletin frequently of late ... I always scan closely the columns "Their Victory Won," and "Missing in Action," for news of any of our son's friends, so many of whom have been listed in these columns recently, a tragic role, yet a role of honor!

Very Sincerely Yours,
Clinton M. Harbison

Bobo Harbison's death was the first tragedy of the war that came really close to us. By the end of the war there would be so many others, old friends, schoolmates, and new friends. I still have the memory of them so young and beautiful and strong. Destroyed. But shocked as we were about Harbison's death, we, none of us, Ned included, were to feel the full impact of it until later, which I'll relate further on.

In the meanwhile the squadron closed ranks and carried on. But they were not so joyous or carefree as before. The laughter was stilled.

It was soon after Harbison's death that Ned began having a strange skin eruption that was to cover his whole body and cause him ultimately to be hospitalized. He had had a small cut which didn't heal, as cuts often don't in the tropics. He went to the medics who applied salicylic acid to his skin and gave him sulfa drugs, which were the wonder drugs of the era—this was long before penicillin. Ned's reaction was bad. His entire body was covered with hives, probably from the sulfa, and a fungus spread out of control from the cut. He was oozing pus from several parts of his body including his ears.

In January, three months after the original cut, they sent him to the Navy hospital in Samoa. "We watched them take old Eddie off on a stretcher and put him in the meat wagon," Coggin recalls. "We were scared when we saw him go. We had seen too many who didn't return."

When the medics in Samoa saw him they wanted to send him immediately to the States, but Ned insisted on trying to get well so he could go back to his squadron. The medical records sent to me by the Marine Corps show that the first step was to quit the sulfa and salicylic acid and to apply "cold wet boric packs two hours in the morning" followed by a lotion of glycerin, calamine, and zinc oxide. He was also washed with a boric wash and boric powder was blown into his ears. Within a week the records show that the disease was under control:

    12 Jan. 1944: improvement
    17 Jan. 1944: very much improved
    19 Jan. 1944: skin cleared entirely
    20 Jan. 1944: discharged to duty. Well.

He was back with his friends just in time to move northward with them. The allied push toward Japan was speeding up and as more and more island bases were wrested from the Japanese, the fighting moved closer and closer to the goal—Tokyo.

In November 1943, the fight to regain the Gilbert Islands had begun with the cruel battle for Tarawa. A thousand of our men were killed and 2,000 wounded, but the island was taken and bases established there. The allied forces were another step nearer Japan. Ned's group was moved from Wallis Island to Funafuti atoll in the Ellice Islands, which lie just south of the Gilberts.

From the Gilberts our forces were able to attack the Japanese bases in the Marshalls, and by February 1944, Kwajalein, the center of the Japanese defenses, was taken at ruinous cost to the Japanese. A month

Pilots just before takeoff. Senhauser is second from left. Ned is on the extreme right.

later, in March 1944, Ned's squadron was sent to the Marshalls, where they were based on Engebi, one of the islands of the almost perfect circle of islands that make up the Eniwetok Atoll. From Eniwetok they were moved to Roi and to Kwajalein and then back to Eniwetok. Assaults on Japanese-held islands increased, and as our forces got nearer and nearer to Japan, bombing missions were routine.

Though it was clear the Japanese could not hold out much longer, it was also clear that they would not change their strategy of fighting to the last man. No one knew how long this would be, but our strength was increasing, not diminishing, so we knew we would carry on.

In August 1944, Ned, Bill Senhauser, and a few others were assigned to return to the States for further training. They were to leave on August 11 from Eniwetok and were elated. But they were to be on duty until the last moment.

On August 4, 1944, at 6 A.M. the alarm sounded—an alert that Japanese planes and ships were heading toward them. Immediate orders were given. Certain dive bombers and fighters were to line up immediately ready to take off and intercept the Japanese. All other pilots were to

Bombers in the Pacific

Bill Senhauser in front of his plane which he named after his Alma Mater

Marshall Coggin (front) and Ned leaving for a two man patrol in their planes. Note Mae West jackets and plotting board that Ned is carrying. Tents in background are where the pilots slept. (March 1944)

clear the base of all aircraft as soon as the first group left.

The fighters were lined up in an area behind the bombers. All men were in their planes or next to them ready for the signal. The fighters would go first. Senhauser and Hultgren were side by side in their bombers—ready. The fighters took off. There was a sudden terrible crash and explosion. Hultgren watched in horror.

Right next to him a fighter, attempting to take off, had crashed into Senhauser's plane. The two planes were engulfed in flames. Senhauser was in the center. His gunner, not yet in the plane, was just far enough away to escape.

Hultgren ran to Senhauser. Senhauser came out of the flames. "He was alive and conscious," Hultgren says. "They took him away to the hospital. It was 6:30 A.M. By 11 he was dead. Every pore in his body

Bill Senhauser, killed August 4, 1944

had been seared closed. They buried him in the military cemetery nearby."

> The flight of another pilot is over, his battles are all fought, his
> victories are all won, and as in other days, he lies down to rest
> while under the arching sky awaiting the bugle call.
>
> *From the memorial service for*
> *William Evans Senhauser*

ﾞ

Five days later four sobered men, Hultgren, Coggin, Filkins, and Dart,
sailed away from Eniwetok toward Pearl harbor. From Pearl Harbor they
were put aboard the SS Sea Marlin for the States.

There was one last service they could perform for their friends who were left behind. Ned was to perform it for Bobo Harbison and Bill Senhauser. It was to change his life.

He was to go to the parents and return their sons' personal effects. He went first to the Harbisons in Lexington, Kentucky. Major and Mrs. Harbison met him at the bus station in downtown Lexington. They drove him up Winchester Pike, through the beautiful blue grass country to the gates of their place and up the quarter-mile driveway to their fine red brick empty house.

"Bobo's parents were two of the saddest people I've ever seen," Ned told us later. "Alone in that big house. Bowed down with grief. Bobo was all they had and he was gone. They clung to me as one last link to their son."

Mrs. Harbison, Bobo's mother, before her marriage was Dorothea Mann, the daughter of an Episcopal bishop in one of the Dakotas. When the United States entered the first world war in 1917, she was in her thirties. She was single and a registered nurse. She was sweet looking but not pretty. She enlisted and was sent to France.

Clinton Harbison, Bobo's father, was the handsome, brilliant son of a prominent Kentucky family. He was a bachelor and a staunch Episcopalian. He had finished law school and had already started a promising career when war broke out. He enlisted and became an officer in the field artillery. He was sent to France.

Dorothea Mann and Clinton Harbison, now Major Harbison, met, fell in love, and were married. They returned to Lexington where he resumed his practice of law. They were older than most newlyweds of the time—he was 32 and she was somewhat older, but to their great joy in 1920 they had a baby boy. They named him Clinton.

By then the father, who was always called Major Harbison, was well on his way to becoming one of the most distinguished lawyers in Lexington. The firm he started still bears his name though he is long since dead.

Like so many parents of only children, especially older parents, the Harbisons cherished their son and gave lavishly to him. But he was not overprotected nor was he spoiled. He was a fine athlete and according to his friends, daring, and always ready for action. He was exceptionally good natured and given to ready laughter. He had a cousin, Shelby Harbison, the son of Major Harbison's brother, who loved to be near young Clint, as everyone called him.

"I idolized my cousin," Shelby Harbison says. "He was four years older than I, strong and handsome—a football player, and he was as nice to younger kids like me as he was to everyone.

"He was very popular. His parents were a little straightlaced but he certainly was not.

"He loved horses, and in 1931 they bought the farm on Winchester Pike—100 acres—and they built the big red brick house there. Clint became an expert polo player and won a lot of silver trophies. His parents were so proud of him.

"They adored him. I saw them soon after they heard the news—they were alone in the big house. Aunt Dorothea was devastated. She was never quite the same afterward. Sad somehow."

Though a year had passed between Bobo's death and Ned's arrival in Lexington with his personal possessions, Major and Mrs. Harbison begged him for any information he could give about their son, about his life and his death.

"They hung on to every word," Ned said, "and I could tell them so little." Still they clung to him, grasping for every scrap. They insisted Ned stay for lunch, which he hadn't planned. But finally he had to leave to catch his bus toward Zanesville, Ohio. Mrs. Harbison drove him to the bus station.

When he got on the bus, she got on too. She simply could not let this last link to her son go.

"She stayed on the bus for almost an hour. We were thirty miles outside of Lexington when she at last asked the bus driver to let her off."

The bus drove off. "I saw her walking back all alone on that long road." He watched as her figure grew smaller and smaller.

"I could see she was weeping," he said. He didn't know it, but that moment marked the turning point for him. He told Mother he could never forget the picture of that broken-hearted woman left on the road as the bus moved on. He was never the same again.

He continued on his way to Zanesville to see Senhauser's mother and deliver Bill's last personal effects. She was Marguerite Senhauser Raymond. She had divorced her first husband, Bill's father, an alcoholic, and had remarried.

When Ned arrived, Wilma Plansoen was there. She was Bill's fiancee, the girl we had met in New Orleans. She and Bill had been in the same class at Duke University in Durham, North Carolina. They had graduated together in 1942.

"He was one of the most prominent students at Duke," Wilma says. "He was bright and popular and active in university politics—a natural leader—and a marvelous dancer." He was also exceptionally handsome. She and Bill had planned to be married during his first leave; Ned was to have been best man.

"I was excited when I got a telephone call from Mrs. Raymond," she says, "I thought it was to say Bill was on his way home and we'd be married. I heard instead that he was dead.

"Then a week or so later, Mrs. Raymond called to say Ed was coming with Bill's things. She wanted me to be with her.

"She was so proud of Bill; he was the one big thing in her life, and the fact that she invited me to come and share this last contact with her son was typical of her. She was big-hearted.

"When I saw her, she was crushed. It was a terrible blow for her. She was grief-stricken, but when Ed came, she composed herself. She was a great lady."

Ned gave Mrs. Raymond Bill's camera, his wallet, and his pictures, including several of Wilma.

"In spite of her grief, or maybe because of it, she asked Ed to stay three or four days. She needed him."

After the visit he was to go to Cherry Point, North Carolina, for his next assignment, but he had a few extra days during which he went to see

Mother and Dad who were vacationing in New England. They had just sold the house at 1803 Jefferson Avenue in New Orleans and were taking a well-earned vacation away from the heat at the Dartmouth Inn in Hanover, New Hampshire.

After seeing the family he passed through New York on his way south and he called Wilma who lived with her family in Nutley, New Jersey. They had dinner together. While he was at Cherry Point in September 1944, they began writing to each other.

Early in October he was transferred to Glenview Naval Air Station in Glenview, Illinois. On October 6 I saw him for the first time since May 1943. It had been a year and a half but it seemed more like a decade.

My husband, Jack, was overseas on a tanker in the Pacific. We had a baby almost a year old, and like so many women my age, I was dividing my time between my parents and my parents-in-law. My husband's parents, John and Evelyn McCutcheon, lived in Lake Forest, Illinois, about twenty miles from Glenview.

Ned was there a whole month, but I saw him only that one time in October when Mother, Dad, and Ninette arrived for a historic family reunion at the McCutcheons'. Luckily my mother-in-law took some snapshots, one of which shows Ned pushing the baby, Anne McCutcheon, whom we called Pandy, in her stroller. He was to ask for a copy of that picture later just before leaving for his second tour of duty overseas and he kept it with him the whole time. Pandy was later to have such admiration for her uncle that she doubtlessly was influenced by him in her choice of architecture as a profession, and I think he admired her. The 1944 snapshot was still among his belongings when he died.

Early in the new year, February, 1945, he was sent to Quantico, Virginia, and then back again to Cherry Point. He was training with a squadron flying a new bomber called a Hell Diver. The training lasted eight months and during that time he had continued his correspondence with Wilma and managed to get leave to see her a couple of times. Before shipping out he was given leave and went to New Orleans for a few days. Then he was flown to San Diego to await orders.

His first letter to the family after his visit was written on the plane.

Ned, Pandy, Mother, Ninette, Dad, Susan, October 6, 1944

Sunday

13 May 1945

Dear Folks—

Here I am on the last leg of my trek westward. We've just crossed the Sierras and are now high over the Mojave desert which stretches for miles below us. It's quite an impressive sight...

I wanted so much to have some prints made of the photo Mrs. M. took of me and Pandy in L.F. last fall. I think it is really very very good and I'd like to give one to Wilma. Would you please send it to me pronto, in your first letter so I can get to work on it. If we wait too long there's a possibility of my leaving before it comes. So please please sent it on.

That's about all for now—I'll wire when I arrive—Love to all—

Ned

Ned with his neice Pandy, who later was influenced enough by him to become an architect

As it turned out he wasn't to leave for a long time because it was just then that the push toward Japan was gaining momentum and the military didn't want to send out any more men than necessary.

Iwo Jima had already fallen after a horrible battle. The island was so strongly defended that in spite of heavy bombardment by B-24s and B-25s and a murderous pre-assault barrage by the Navy, it took 30,000 Marines over a month to triumph—March 26, 1945. But the cost was high. Seven thousand of our men were dead.

The Japanese had lost 22,000 but they wouldn't give up, even though everyone, including themselves, knew that the end was in sight. When it would come, no one knew. Thus Ned and his squadron hung around San Diego for two months waiting for orders.

His letters to the family during that time, most of which survive, are a clear indication of the change that had come over him—still the same bonhomie, but less reckless and more in command of himself. He is also more in command of his orthography and grammar.

Wednesday
30 May 1945

Dear Mom,

Thanks so much for your birthday greetings and for the present Dad gave me [he was 23 on May 28] ... Of course the day proved as unexciting as the three previous birthdays ... a day of reckoning will come. Let's hope shortly.

Still we're in some doubt as to when we sail. I'm sure it will be before the end of June and have a good idea maybe before the 15th of that month. We never know, but rest assured I'll let you know when we're "hot" or ready to leave as the expression goes.

He tells of meeting an old classmate from the University of Virginia just back from Iwo Jima, who, in his words:

> brought the sad news that my old pal Joe Bottalico was killed not long ago on Iwo. You must remember my talking of Joe, the Italian boy from Camden, N.J. Gee, more of the old gang have been lost.

It's at this time that his first interest in art is mentioned:

> I went into town the other day and went wild in an art store. Bought drawing board, pens, ink, paper, etc. etc. in an effort to learn how to letter properly. My amateurish work is displayed on this envelope. They say with practice you improve—so I'm practicing like mad. There's ink all over the place—I think more on me than on the paper. Same old Ned.

Another trait begins to show itself. It is his determination to stand up to Mother, especially now that he and Wilma were talking of marriage. She was set on making good Catholics of all of us, but he was not going to let her run his life.

> Mother, I've been thinking lots about your visit, in the near future, with Wilma, especially in regard to your decision to bring

up the painful subject of religion. Knowing Wilma as I do, her convictions etc. I was wondering if you'd refrain from even bringing it up, or if you really want to, touch on it very lightly. You see, I don't want this first meeting to be fouled up in any way and maybe it will be unpleasant for both of you. We discuss it in every letter, looking at it in every possible way and, though she's never mentioned it, I know we want to figure it out for ourselves unaided or uninfluenced by either side. It's such a ticklish subject! Do you understand how I feel? I know you won't make any demands or put her in the "squeeze," its just that the very mentioning of it will make her feel more on the spot than she will ordinarily. Both of us know very well what's in store for us either way. Let us solve it our way! Please Mom, do this for me? I should have asked you this when I was home, for when you first mentioned it I didn't like the idea, but I didn't. Then too she may think I asked you to try and influence her. That's unfair—so please make this first meeting as pleasant as possible and leave religion out of it.

He wasn't shipped out in June after all, and with time on his hands, his interest and proficiency in art increased.

7 June 1945

Dear Folks—

It doesn't seem as if we'll ever pull out of here. Gee, I'm so tired of sitting around doing nothing. I want to hurry up and get it all over with so I can come home all that much quicker. From recent indications we may still be here next week and maybe the next—who knows?

We received two more shots today. Cholera and Typhus. Lord, if they inject any more serum into me I think I'll be immune to everything possible. Thyphus, Thyphoid, Tetanus, Cholera and Cowpox. Can you think of many more? As a result I feel awful tonite, but nothing that a good nite's rest won't cure.

Life is so dull out here, I have all kinds of time to devote to drawing and lettering. It's lots of fun for me and educational at the same time. Did I tell you I had written Yale and stated my case, hoping to get some idea as to what to expect.

Soon thereafter he hears from the dean of Yale School of Architecture with encouraging news that he would be eligible to apply for admission.

> I'm excited as all get out. He [the dean] wanted my transcript from W.F.S. and Va. Oh brother, wait till he sees my charming record at the latter.

In the same letter (June 19, 1945) the thorny subject of religion comes up again:

> Received your letter on religion sometime ago and haven't answered it mainly because I've said "well I'll do it tomorrow." I don't like to discuss that delicate subject in letters because I feel I can't express myself as well as in person—that's why I've let it go. Anyway, I'm sorry you took my previous letter so hard. It wasn't meant to be—but I can't seem to discuss that subject nowadays without violent repercussions on the home front.

There is no more mention of religion. Mother got the message. In his next letters it's clear he plans to marry Wilma a soon as he returns and without parental interference of any kind.

On July 9, 1945, he writes:

> Well, we're finally leaving! I can't say the date but real soon. So I'll be gone for another year unless the good Lord ends this hell for us sooner. There will be a delay of quite some time en route so don't expect any mail for some time.

They shipped out on July 18, 1945, on the USS Barnwell. Elm Filkins, J. J. Hultgren, and Ned were still together. They arrived in the Admiralty Islands, north of New Guinea on August 14. They were at sea when the atom bomb was dropped on Hiroshima on August 6 and another on Nagasaki on August 9.

August 15, 1945

Dear Folks—

Well, we've finally arrived at our destination and even though we're still in the transient unsettled state at this point, it is awful good to be on land again after our long voyage [almost a month at sea].

This is going to be short as usual as we're still en route. Let me retract my first statement. This is the destination of our ship but not our own. Confusing isn't it?

But who gives a hoot!! Today we learned the news of the Japanese surrender. The war is over!! I find it quite hard to believe it now and then, and generally I feel as if I'm still dreaming. Isn't it grand tho! No more killing and homecoming isn't, can't be, too far away. With the danger element removed time is my only enemy now and that makes me very happy. I can see the delighted expression on your faces when they said the happy news. We were on board ship at the time of the first Jap offer and my excitement reached its peak since last August when I saw the Golden Gate after 12 months overseas. Ain't it grand?

Upon arrival, there was no mail waiting for us as I had expected. It has gotten fouled up as usual and is at another island . . .

Must go. Address on front. Please write. Love to all—

Your boy
Ned

Ned, August 1945

After the surrender the main object was to get home as soon as possible. Ned was shipped home, but by slow stages. He landed in Hawaii on August 28, 1945, and by sheer good luck he met Harry. They hadn't seen each other since 1942. His letter is dated the same day.

> August 28, 1945
>
> Great news! I saw Harry today and we spent a very pleasant afternoon renewing our acquaintance. Gee its been a long time, but I felt as if we were sitting on the back porch at 1803 instead of out here. He looks fine—a little thin but he's fine. I beefed about the USMC and good ole H. griped about the army. Boy it was fun! Definitely, the Dart brothers hate war with a passion which could never be put down in words. The problem is, when oh when will we be civilians once more?
>
> He met me at the gate of my base and we went over to his camp. Over some cokes and a few highballs we brought back memories and how I know you, Neen, Susy and Dad would have loved to have been there and how we would have loved to have you there. Someday tho we'll have a big re-union.
>
> H. may get to go home soon. Of course he doesn't know, but I think it's in the bag. As for me, I only wish I could say the same. From all indications I won't be home for some time.
>
> Are you still in Hanover? I got one letter (the first) today and it was dated July 23 so you see I'm way behind the times. Let me tell you though, it was really super to read all my mail this morning. Got nine from Wilma and there's lots more to come as soon as it finishes traveling all over the Pacific—maybe tomorrow.
>
> Harry & I are getting together again tomorrow afternoon and I think we'll have dinner together over here. Our mess is lots better than his anyway.
>
> So you see its been quite exciting for me after being so dejected for six lonesome weeks en route. g'nite for now!
>
> Love
> *Neddo*

Harry, who was five years older than Ned and entirely different in temperament and interests, was nevertheless very fond of his younger brother. As children, Harry used to let Ned chase him—both were good runners and both were to distinguish themselves on their school and college track teams.

As they grew up, except for the summer of 1937 when they went to the ranch in Arizona, they spent less and less time together. They were both away at school—Harry graduated from Princeton in 1939 when Ned still had a year to go at Woodberry Forest, and Ned rarely wrote to anyone except Mother. When they were both overseas she tried to keep each of them up to date on news from the other, to the extent that she was able.

It was sheer luck that Ned saw Harry in Hawaii. Harry was stationed at the Army's anti-aircraft headquarters on Oahu, and Ned was en route home. He just happened to land at the Marine Corps air station at Ewa.

He apparently knew that Harry was somewhere in the Hawaiian Islands, but he had no idea exactly where. Since bomber pilots were no longer needed in the Pacific, Harry knew Ned would be going home, but he had no idea when or via what route. It was a total surprise when he heard Ned's voice on the phone. Harry tells of their meeting on a tape recording he made recently of his wartime experiences.

> I got this call from Ned, and he told me where he was located— at Barracks number so and so and I said I'll be right over.
>
> When I got over there I asked him, "How the hell did you find out where I was?"
>
> "Well," he said, "I was walking down the road, and I saw a couple of Navy flyers and I just took a chance and went up to them and told them I had a brother in the anti-aircraft artillery in the Army and asked if they knew where the headquarters were.
>
> "One of these two Navy guys asked his name and when I said Harry Dart, he said, 'Harry Dart. We know him well. Yeah, he's right down the road there.'"

It was one of the good fortunes of war that the only two Navy flyers Harry knew in the entire Pacific were the two Ned encountered.

It was at this meeting with Ned that Harry was the first to learn of

Ned's proficiency in art. He tells of it on tape.

> He had been painting an oil painting—or was it a water color?
> I can't remember. He had it pinned up on the wall opposite his
> bunk. It was a still life, and he looked at that thing and he took
> a bowie knife and swung it and the knife went right through the
> middle of that picture. The knife stuck into the wooden wall of
> the barracks.
>
> I said, "What did you do that for?" He said, "Aw, I don't like
> that." And then he opened his footlocker and pulled out a sheaf
> of beautiful pen and ink drawings and oils—gosh, beautiful
> pictures. Very professional. I said, "Gee, where did you buy
> those? In Australia?"
>
> "Buy them? I did these myself."
>
> I said, "My God, what are you going to do with this?"
>
> Well, he said the first thing he was going to do was to go to New
> Jersey and marry Wilma. And then the second thing he was
> going to do was to go into either commercial art or architecture.
>
> Well, as you know he soon decided to go into architecture and
> he applied for entrance into the School of Architecture at Yale,
> and offered the same sheaf of pictures that he had shown me.
> Now, as you know, architecture is a grad school. He had two
> miserable years at University of Virginia with a terrible record,
> but with that sheaf of pictures he had no trouble.
>
> That was his passport to get into architecture school. Anybody
> who looked at those pictures could tell this guy was something
> of a genius.

It may have been on the basis of the art work, or possibly the dearth
of students throughout the war, that Yale School of Architecture admitted
Ned. But before he started, like everyone else he had to be demobilized.

In October and November of 1945 we saw the flood tide of returning
soldiers, sailors, and Marines. They were everywhere, and rejoicing was
the dominant mood. My heart went out to those who returned blind or
paralyzed or crippled—and to their families, and to the families of those
who never returned.

I could never celebrate the end of the war. It has, in a sense, never ended for me. I think only of our terrible loss. I think of:

Lucien Lyons, one of my favorite dancing partners, handsome with dark hair and fair skin. A lieutenant instructor in the Army Air Force stationed in California. Plane explosion. *Killed January 7, 1943.*

Jerry Thomas, a schoolmate at the Newman School, brother of my friend Sister Thomas. An only son. Captain in the Air Force stationed in North Africa. Plane crash over the Mediterranean. *Killed June 13, 1943.*

Pierre Gelpi, son of our family doctor, handsome and bright. A fighter pilot in the Navy, just turned twenty-one and about to leave for overseas. His mother, a good friend of our mother, waiting to hear that he had arrived at his port of embarkation. A telegram from the Navy instead. Practice flight at high altitude. Oxygen failure. *Killed September 9, 1943.*

Paul Thomson, my classmate at Newman from third grade until he went to VMI and became a Marine captain. He was in the assault force that stormed the beach at Saipan. *Killed June 16, 1944.*

Bobby Hart, whom I knew in childhood and who always danced with me at parties. Eighth Air Force. Shot down over France. *Killed August 8, 1944.*

Gayle Aiken, the laughing, blond headed boy across the street, who had joined the Coast Guard and had come to see me at Connecticut College while he was in training in New London. Assigned as executive officer on an ammunition ship, the USS Serpens. Blown up in Guadalcanal harbor by a two-man Japanese suicide submarine. *Killed January 29, 1945.*

Russell Clark, an only son, a lieutenant in Naval aviation. Shot down by enemy aircraft in the Pacific. *Killed August 24, 1945.*

I grieve when I think of them. We have not forgotten.

❧

Ned finally arrived in San Diego in October 1945. He got forty-three days leave plus travel time and on January 17, 1946, he was relieved from active duty. Two days later he married Wilma. Elm Filkins was the best man.

CHAPTER FOUR

❧

ARCHITECTURE

EDWARD DART, ARCHITECT

Ned and Wilma were married on January 19, 1946. "My family was as pro-Protestant as Ed's mother was pro-Catholic," Wilma says. "My parents [Anna and Leonard Plansoen] were Dutch. They had emigrated from Zeeland, but originally my father's family was French. The name was Plançon. They were French Huguenots who left France in the seventeenth century. My mother and father knew each other in Holland but were not married until they came to this country—the day after she arrived."

The Plansoens lived on the east coast, ultimately settling in New Jersey where Leonard Plansoen was a building contractor and where Wilma and her brother John grew up. She went to high school in Belleville and on to Duke University in North Carolina where she graduated in 1942. The following year she went to Katherine Gibbs Secretarial School in New York, which was to stand her in good stead during the lean years to come. She also taught Sunday school in the Congregational Church.

I wasn't at Ned's and Wilma's wedding and it is one of the great regrets of my life. Neither were Mother and Ninette. Only Dad was present in the church, though Mother and Ninette went to the reception afterward. My not being present was unavoidable as I was out of the country at the McCutcheon island in the Bahamas.

Mother's and Ninette's not being present was due to a stupid mistake. Mother had been told that a Catholic could not go to the wedding of another Catholic unless a priest were performing the sacrament. To have done so, she was told, would be tantamount to approving an illegitimate marriage and therefore a sin.

Wilma Plansoen Dart on her wedding day

Whether she believed that or whether she was simply being self-righteous, I don't know. After the wedding a good friend and staunch Catholic told her she could easily have found an open-minded and kind-hearted priest to give her a dispensation. Besides, Ned had already left the fold by then, so Mother and Ninette could have gone on the ground that it was a wedding of two non-Catholics. *Tant pis,* as Grand-mère, who had not much use for the Church, would have said.

In any case, nothing dampened the young couple's spirits. Ned had bought a second-hand car, which he called "Black Magic," and he took Wilma skiing at Lake Placid, New York. "Neither of us had ever skied before," Wilma says, "and we had a wonderful time. Then we went straight to New Haven and began looking for a place to live.

"Our first home was a rented room on the second floor of an old house we called Dirty Ida's. We had kitchen privileges but I was horrified. Being an old Dutchman, I cleaned the oven and refrigerator and insisted that we

Ned and Wilma soon after their wedding

get our own set of dishes. What we yearned for was our own Quonset hut."

Quonset huts, those tunnel-shaped metal structures that served every purpose from housing to storage, were seen everywhere during and after the war. They were developed at Quonset Naval Base in Rhode Island but actually were patterned after the Nissen hut, which the British had used for years. The Nissen hut, which was designed by Lt. Col. Peter Nissen, a World War I Canadian military engineer, was a remarkably efficient answer to the need for quick and cheap shelter or storage. People didn't object to them because they were obviously temporary and sure to be demolished when things returned to normal. They sprang up at campuses and schools all over America to accommodate the thousands of service-men who chose to take advantage of the GI Bill, which paid for tuition but not much else.

In New Haven, where a whole village of Quonset huts had been built, the demand was so great that there was a long waiting list.

"We dreamed of what we'd do when we got ours," Wilma says. "We stayed at Dirty Ida's a year before our dream—our first home—came true.

"We loved it. The huts were divided into two living units, each with its own entrance at opposite ends of the hut. Our address was 244-A Whitney Avenue. We spent two years there and I still keep up with the couple who lived in the other half. All of the families were ex-servicemen on the GI Bill—some already had babies."

The interior of the Dart hut was destined for great changes. It started as nothing more than a plywood floor with a partition around a makeshift bathroom and another around a bedroom. The kitchen was nothing but a stove, fridge, and sink in the main room.

"After we fixed it up we thought it was wonderful," Wilma says. "My father, who was good at carpentry, came up and built a beautiful cabinet between the stove and the rest of the hut so we had a separate living-dining room. I put yellow curtains in the windows. We had an old daybed that I had slipcovered, one chair, one table, and one lamp. Our bedroom was so small we hardly had room for a double bed, but somehow Ed built a drafting table and did his work there."

Ninette stopped by shortly thereafter and sent home a report, "Spic and span clean like old Dutch cleanser," she marvelled. "Once when we were going out, Wilma spent the last few minutes dusting the furniture and waxing the floor with an electric waxing machine. I couldn't get over it. Nobody else I ever knew did that."

Wilma recalls that waxing machine well. "The floors of the Quonset hut were plywood and I wanted waxed floors so we bought a waxing machine and between times we rented it out to others, so in the end we paid for the machine several times over."

Being thrifty was an inborn trait in Wilma. Her secretarial skills were still fresh and she got a job. "I was secretary to the head of the physics department," she says. "And then we also had the sandwich business. We made dozens and dozens every night—baloney, ham, cheese—and we sold them in the dormitories."

Still they could barely make ends meet. They were expecting a baby in the spring of 1948, and Wilma had to give up her job a few months before the baby was due.

"We were so broke we had to sell Black Magic. Ed bought a bike to get to his classes and I walked everywhere."

But the biggest change for Wilma was Ned's attitude, his seriousness of purpose. "As soon as he entered the school of architecture I noticed the big change," she says. "I was suddenly not the first interest in his life. If I had noticed the serious side of his nature before, I was not quite prepared for this complete transition. This time it was all work and positively no play—none whatsoever. I have to admit it was a blow to my vanity. It took me a while to adjust, but when I did, I was the proudest wife on campus."

Ned had never worked so hard in his life. Besides his school work and the sandwich business, he reworked the partitions in the hut so there would be a room for the baby. He had also undertaken his first professional job: he was designing a house for Mother and Dad in Vermont.

After they sold 1803, the house in New Orleans, and took that first trip to Hanover, New Hampshire, they spent summers in houses rented from Dartmouth professors. In 1948 they bought thirty acres in Thetford, Vermont, across the river from Hanover, as the site for their own vacation home.

A letter from Ned tells of his progress.

February 5, 1948

Dear Mother & Dad—

This will be a business letter more or less to keep you informed as to what is happening concerning the house. The fall term ended last week and exams are over and after three days of working my Quonset over in preparation for the new baby I set to work on the final sketches for your house. I've been working like a demon on it and to the joy of everyone concerned it's practically finished. It's been a long fight since last summer when the first idea was conceived and although I did a lot before I saw you at Christmas since then a lot more has been accomplished and the house is taking an air of refinement which to me is extremely satisfying. The complete composition came to me the other night—that is the realization of what I wanted to do became clear—and for the first time I knew for certain that what I had drawn was a happy solution to the problem.

On March 21 their daughter, Elaine Dupaquier Dart, was born. She was a fine, healthy baby. "But we really needed a car," Wilma says. "We finally bought an old roadster with a rumble seat. It looked grand, but the first time we took it out the engine, or something like that, fell out. We went back to biking and walking."

In the meanwhile Ned was making progress at Yale, where he had the good fortune to study under some of the most eminent architects practicing in America. They came as visiting professors on a six-week rotating program. Among them during Ned's years at Yale were Pietro Belluschi, Marcel Breuer, Harwell Hamilton Harris, Richard Neutra, Louis Kahn, Eero Saarinen, Harold Spitznagel, Edward Durell Stone, and Paul Schweikher. Richard M. Bennett was chairman of the department of architecture as well as a professor of design. Stone was to figure somewhat in Ned's later career, and Schweikher and Bennett were to figure prominently in it.

By the end of the year, the house in Vermont was well under way. His letter dated December 17 tells of a visit there.

> I didn't arrive at the house last Wednesday until 9 p.m. Bill [the carpenter] took me in and it is quite terrific to enter your house at night with all the lights on. He had practically finished the ceiling in the living-dining-kitchen area and it is beautiful. The entrance door is hung and I can't tell you how sweet it looks. It would be a crime to paint it, you'll see ...
>
> Bill is starting on the seat in the living room next week. He had sanded the rough flooring preparatory to laying the finished floor which he will do shortly. As cold as it was yesterday the little house was as snug and warm even without ducts connected to the heater. Of course we had a roaring fire going all day ... Mother you will be knocked out by its charm—just between us I think it is a lovely thing that you may be justly proud of.

Architectural drawing of Vermont house (1949)

Vermont house, viewed from the side (1949)

Interior of the Vermont house (1949)

1989 view of the Vermont house (Doris Lingelbach photo)

The house was finished in 1949 and proved a source of great joy to all of us. It was fresh and new and clean; it was the essence of what we wanted after the turmoil of the war. In some ways it represented the best that architecture was to bring in the 1950s. In others it embodied the worst that developers and, alas, architects were to inflict upon us.

It was made of natural wood and stone, inside and out, with an enormous fireplace of field stone in the living room and big glass windows looking out on the mountains. It fitted into its setting like a bird nesting on a hilltop. Unbound by heavy traditional concepts, it gave a feeling of light and freedom outside and warmth and snugness inside.

But it was not an unqualified success. Its most conspicuous flaw was that, like so many other post-war houses in America, the garage was placed right smack in front—a rotten idea under any circumstances and totally unnecessary in this one. Another fault is the exaggerated off-center slant of the roof, a fad that was so overdone by cheap builders that it became a cliché of the 50s.

But in spite of these flaws the house was and still is, on balance, a good house, partly because of the love that was lavished on it. Mother furnished it with Shaker-like simplicity—plain New England furniture stripped down to the bare wood with only a hand-rubbed finish. And she kept it so neat and clean that it took on an air of elegance.

I visited there many times with our children, and to this day they remember the house with fondness. Our daughter Mary McCutcheon, who spent a whole summer there at age ten says, "I always loved that house. It was a happy house and I was happy there." And Harry's daughter Charlotte liked it so much as a child that she seriously thought of moving her family from New Orleans to Vermont a quarter of a century later.

In the spring of 1949, not long after the house was finished, Ned was graduated from Yale School of Architecture. He had offers from two of the architects who had taught him, Edward Durell Stone in New York and Paul Schweikher in Roselle, Illinois. On May 11 he came to see Schweikher. That visit clinched the deal. He stayed overnight with Jack and me in Lake Forest, and the next morning I drove him to Roselle for the interview. Winston Elting was Schweikher's partner at the time, and they offered him a job. He accepted on the spot.

On the way back we stopped at the Lloyd Lewis house in Libertyville designed by Frank Lloyd Wright. I knew the Lewises but did not know that Lloyd Lewis had just died. Luckily Dorothy Aldis, my neighbor and a good friend of the Lloyd Lewises, was there helping out while Katherine Lewis was out, so she showed us the house, a beautiful example of Wright architecture. Ned was impressed.

The next day he had a few hours to spare before leaving, and I asked him what he wanted to do.

"I want to see more Wright houses," he said. "I know there are several on the North Shore, and if you can drive me to them, that's all I ask."

We started by going south on Sheridan Road and stopping at the Willitts house in Highland Park. We knocked on the door but were sent packing in no uncertain terms.

A few minutes later we saw a house in Glencoe on the west side of Sheridan Road overlooking a ravine (850 North Sheridan Road), and as we were crossing the bridge, Ned said, "Stop. I think that's one there. I can smell Wright."

A woman answered the door. It was still early in the morning, and at first she hesitated (Wright house owners are pestered all the time by sight-seers), but two such eager young pilgrims must have softened her heart. She let us in and as Ned showed such obvious appreciation, she let us see more and more of the house—even the bedrooms with unmade beds and the back hall where a litter of pups had recently been born—until we had seen the whole house.

"That was wonderful," Ned said to the owner as we were leaving. And he meant it.

We saw one or two other Wright houses from the outside. If I'm not mistaken we saw the Hiram Baldwin house at 205 Essex Road in Kenilworth and the Baker house at 507 Lake Avenue in Wilmette. He was very happy, and there is no doubt that Wright's work was to influence his own later on.

When he later returned to Illinois, he began the difficult task of locating a place to live within his slender means. He found an apartment in Itasca, Illinois, not too far from Schweikher's office and began working immediately. Wilma and Elaine were to follow a week or so later. In the meanwhile he asked to use our garage in which to build a crib for Elaine. I had never known anyone who had built a crib for a baby. After all a crib didn't cost much. But Ned had to be thrifty. What delighted me was the way he went about it. The design was as simple as could be and the workmanship was elegant, yet it cost less than the cheapest crib.

"If I can't make it as an architect," he told me as he was sawing the wood, "I'll be a carpenter." But making it as an architect was clearly his goal. He took his work with Schweikher and Elting seriously, and he signed up for his licensing exams as early as he possibly could. He passed them on the first try.

In the meanwhile, he had begun looking for a house he could afford. By scouting around he found an unused tumbledown log cabin on the grounds of a fairly nice house on Old Plum Grove Road in Palatine not far from his work. He reached an agreement with the owner to fix up the place in exchange for living there rent free. What he failed to do was specify how long the agreement would last.

The owner watched while he used all his talents and all his strength to transform that cabin into one of the most charming little dwellings I've ever seen. I remember marveling at what he and Wilma had accomplished. Besides the carpentry and repairing the wiring and plumbing, he had cleaned out a well and Wilma had scrubbed and waxed until the place shone. It was only a short time before the owner gave notice for them to move.

Disappointed but undaunted, they found a small farm cottage on the grounds of Dr. Melvin Thompson's place in Barrington for rent at a modest rate. Thompson, a dentist, and his wife became good friends of the Darts, who lived there happily for over a year.

On Friday, October 7, 1949, I got a call from Ned, which I carefully recorded in my diary. "How would you like to go up to Spring Green, Wisconsin, tomorrow and meet Frank Lloyd Wright?" he asked. I jumped at the chance and hastily made arrangements to have someone look after the children, as Jack, at that time a reporter for the *Chicago*

Tribune, worked on Saturdays. We set off early the next day in the car that Ned had bought recently.

Spring Green, near Madison, is about a four-hour drive from Lake Forest. It seems that there was some sort of architects' convention in Chicago, and Wright invited them up to Taliesin. Taliesin is named after the legendary Welsh bard, and for Wright, with his Welsh background, it was a fitting name. When we arrived we remarked that the ancient name was particularly fitting also because of the decrepit buildings, glorious in their disrepair.

In this sense it was like "Falling Water," the house Wright designed beside a waterfall in Bear Run, Pennsylvania, which has falling water indoors as well as outdoors. Wright's expertise did not always extend to watertight roofs. (Neither did Ned's, alas.)

Regardless of its tatty appearance, Taliesin is as inspiring a place as Falling Water. At every turn you see an exciting roof line or a beckoning vista. Indoors the rooms with their low doorways and arresting details can engage a visitor for a long time. Ned was entranced.

He wandered off somewhere while Wilma and I were resting and waiting outside by one of the main buildings. We didn't mind as it was a warm day with plenty of things to look at and plenty of people to watch. You can imagine how every architect (not to mention their wives and sisters) for miles around had taken advantage of Wright's really very generous invitation. After a half hour or so, Ned reappeared looking mighty pleased.

"The Master spoke to me," he exclaimed with mock excitement, but it was clear that his excitement wasn't all fake.

"He did?" we said. "What did he say to you?"

"He said, 'Put out that cigarette. We neither smoke nor wear hats in the buildings.' Then he turned around and walked away with his hat squarely on his head."

We stayed until late afternoon looking at the buildings and talking to the apprentice-students (some people called them serfs) who were going about their tasks as usual. There was a movie theater with ghastly Russian movies of ink blots and blobs of color that moved about the screen to the sound of bizarre music. We searched in vain for a plot or even a message, and soon gave up.

Wright was on hand as we left, unsmiling in his broad brimmed hat. We shook his hand as we thanked him, but he just looked at us and didn't say anything.

Paul Schweikher had a great influence on Ned's work. The architectural office was in the Schweikher home in Roselle, and Ned took me there several times. It was a house he loved. The interior was of natural wood, and the built-in seating in the living room had soft grey-blue upholstered cushions. I thought then, and still think, that the combination of natural wood and dusty blue is restful and pleasing to the eye.

Paul Schweikher was a grand person and Ned admired him enormously. Soon after he went to work for Schweikher, Ned was assigned to a big project that required extreme accuracy. There was also a deadline. After working on it all week, Ned discovered late Friday that he had made a mistake of a quarter of an inch on a crucial measurement that threw out every subsequent measurement. His entire week's work had to be scrapped. All weekend he agonized over whether he should offer to forego his pay for the week when he told Schweikher of his error. It was the upright thing to do, but he needed the money badly. When Monday came and he confessed his error, he said he'd forego his wage, but Paul Schweikher acted like the prince he was. He wouldn't hear of cutting Ned's pay and excused the mistake simply as a human error.

In spite of his admiration for Schweikher, it wasn't long before Ned was chafing at the bit. "I've got to design," he told me once with desperation in his voice. Some time in 1950, reluctant as he was to leave Schweikher, he opened his own office in his home.

He did this on the strength of a possible commission to design a house for Hope and Phil Stewart off Waukegan Road in Lake Forest. Hope and Phil were looking for an architect with new ideas and heard of Ned through friends of mine. The Stewarts took to him instantly and engaged him to design the house, which he did to their satisfaction.

But soon after the plans were completed, Phil Stewart enlisted in the Army and served in Korea; construction was delayed for three years. To keep the wolf from the door, Ned went to work briefly for Skidmore Owings and Merrill in Chicago. It was a lean few months. Wilma got a temporary job working by the hour picking apples in an apple orchard, and one day Ned came to me and asked if he could borrow $20 for groceries, which he paid back next pay day. They never gave up.

He hated working for someone else, and he quit SOM as soon as he could. He worked there only a few months because it so happened that Jack and Joan Karstrom, friends of the Stewarts, bought land next to the Stewarts and engaged Ned to design their house. At about the same time, a few small projects came his way, all of which helped keep them in groceries. Edward Durell Stone, with whom he had kept in touch since the Yale days, let him design the "House of the Fifties" for *Good Housekeeping* magazine, and probably on the strength of that, he was asked to design a model house for *Popular Mechanics.* There is no evidence that either of them was built.

But plans he drew for a commercial venture called the New Homes Guide were used extensively; no one knows how he got the commission or how many of those houses were built. He barely mentioned these plans to me—he never liked canned plans—but I guess he was desperate enough at the time to justify his acceptance of whatever royalties were offered for the sale of the plans.

"It was a very successful enterprise," Wilma says. "To this day I get calls from all over the country asking for information as to where they can be purchased. It was a great bonus, but Ed disliked the idea and was not too proud of some of the designs, so as soon as our economy improved, he destroyed all evidence."

The Karstrom house was completed in late 1950 or early 1951, and like the family's house in Vermont, it has some of the typical builder's faults of the times—the self-consciously asymmetrical roof line and a general sort of unsubstantial look. But the house still stands and is well cared for. It is at 1300 North Waukegan Road, Lake Forest, Illinois.

Even before the Karstrom house was finished, Ned had begun to think about a house for himself and his family. He bought a lovely five-acre piece of land on Spring Creek Road in Barrington, and we all gathered there—the Darts and the McCutcheons—to view the site and talk of plans for the future—ours and theirs.

We talked of how we wanted to live and what kind of house suited that way of life. It had to be light and airy, uncluttered, and above all, easy to keep up. A place for children and dogs. Jack and I had three children and Wilma was pregnant with her second.

Early that summer of 1951, a baby boy was born and named Edward Louis Dart, but he was sickly. He died when he was two days old and was buried the next day. Only Ned, Wilma, and I were there.

The cemetery was empty except for a few workmen. Ned and Wilma were waiting for me at the grave site. Ned was dressed in a clean white shirt and tie; Wilma and I had on light summer dresses. It was a golden sunshiny morning with birds flying overhead, and the three of us, so young, stood by the newly dug grave with the tiny casket, a simple box, beside it. Ned read some passages of Scripture, the box was lowered into the ground, and a workman standing nearby put a shovelful of soil in the grave. It was the simplest possible ceremony and the most moving. Ned had made the casket himself. The workman was still filling the hole when we left. After the burial Ned went right back to his drawing board, which was in a corner of the rented farm cottage.

Bit by bit his practice grew. In the Spring of 1951 he was awarded a prize of $250 for a pretty little house he entered in the National Association of Home Builders design competition. He also got several jobs for additions and was engaged to design the Interstate Electrical Supply building in Waukegan (completed in 1951 and still standing).

It was on the strength of these commissions that he opened his first office. He rented a room in a shabby building in Highland Park for a month or two and then moved to an upstairs room on Park Avenue across from the railroad station in Barrington. He stayed there only a short time before he established himself in his first real office, 106 East Station Street in Barrington, a five or ten-minute drive from where his own new house was being built on Spring Creek Road (now Braeburn Road).

How many times I put the children in the car after school and took the forty-five minute drive from Lake Forest to Barrington just to see Ned and the house. How we watched with delight as it took shape. It was an exciting moment in our lives. The night before the house was com-

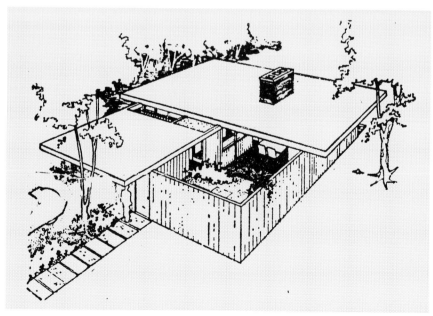

Winner of National Association of Homebuilders competition, 1951

pleted—the windows weren't in yet—Ned and Elaine, who was three years old, spent the night there. It may have been because he had to meet the window installer early the next morning, but more likely it was because he couldn't wait.

It was an elegant little house in spite of—possibly because of—the economic restraints that dictated so many of the architectural solutions. You entered along a severe brick wall that led to a plain wood door. Inside you were greeted by the openness of the living room with big windows looking out to a wide countryside view.

The bedrooms, snug and low, were at the other end of the house with the kitchen and dining area between them and the living room. The kitchen was plain and efficient, open to the dining area, which they furnished with inexpensive ladder back chairs, painted black, and a wooden table that Ned had designed and made—plain, unstained wood with a hand-rubbed finish and butterfly inserts of walnut.

"I still use that as my dining room table," Wilma says, "and I love it for its elegant lines." Ned was to go on designing furniture and fixtures and some of his work—a coffee table of beautiful wood, for example, and a wrought iron chandelier—are still in use.

The Darts and the McCutcheons spent the first Thanksgiving (1951) in the new house. I had gone there the night before so I could help Wilma stuff the turkey. I slept in one of the small cozy bedrooms that had a dutch door leading outside. Waking up in that room was a delightful experience; you were warm and snug inside and yet intimately part of the grass and trees and sky outside.

Early that morning Wilma and I began preparing the feast. We did everything from scratch. We made pies and mashed potatoes. Frozen pies and potatoes from a box were happily not yet available—or if they were, they didn't seduce us. Wilma set the table with simple place mats, dark green napkins, and fall leaves for a centerpiece. When Jack and our children joined us, we were ready for a memorable Thanksgiving.

These details are worth mentioning only because they were so different from the traditional style of eating and sleeping in which we had been raised. This was lighter, easier, more spontaneous.

Architectural drawing for Dart house

*Ned and Wilma's house in Barrington, Illinois
(Hedrich-Blessing photo/Chicago Historical Society Collection)*

Wilma is to be credited as much as Ned for the success of that house. She made the curtains from rough unbleached cotton she had got at cost from a relative in the East. They were unlined pleated draperies, so precisely done that they looked professional. She furnished the house in the same manner—plain and simple. "We had put in a hardwood floor in the living room," she says. "An extravagance—but such a source of pride to both of us. I loved that floor. I waxed it and cherished it.

"Of course we had to improvise in other areas. Do you remember our coffee table? It consisted of a square piece of plywood resting on four large tomato juice cans painted black, and this we covered with an inexpensive square of cloth—madras, I believe. Funny but I remember Mrs. McCutcheon particularly being impressed." Mrs. McCutcheon, my mother-in-law, the daughter of the distinguished architect, Howard Van Doren Shaw, always loved going to the Dart house and always came away impressed by what she had seen. She respected Ned's work.

I can't recall any of the economic compromises Ned and Wilma made that were unattractive or unpleasant except one. Floor covering of any kind was expensive, so the floor, except in the living room, was bare concrete—hard and ugly. Ned painted it a deep red which looked oppressive and was singularly impractical. Every foot mark showed up, and Wilma, for whom cleanliness was next to godliness, had to scrub it so much that the red paint wore off in spots. Scatter rugs helped, but not much. About four years later they put in proper flooring.

"We were as good as the best when we finished," Wilma says. "We carpeted the dining area and put tile in the kitchen and the bathrooms and hardwood floors in the bedrooms.

Even before the floors were redone, there was something about this small house—an architectural philosophy you might say—that was to come to full bloom in Ned's later work. It was joyous in its honesty.

It still stands as I write this in 1992 but is so cluttered and distorted with many additions that when I went back to take photos recently, I was too upset to stay long. It seemed to me that the things we cared so passionately about—the clean design, the simplicity, the freedom of the new way of life—were gone.

From 1951 on Ned's work increased. In 1952 he got his first commission to design a church, St. Michael's Episcopal Church in Barrington, and engaged his first assistant, David Hilles.

"I had known Ed at Yale," Hilles says. "He was two years ahead of me. We met again in Paul Schweikher's office when I went to be interviewed for a job, but by the time I got to Illinois, Ed had his own office in Barrington. A year later I joined Ed in that office.

"We worked on St. Michael's Church and the house for Phil Stewart, and there was another job, a small factory for Henry Pratt. Every morning we'd come in and ask, 'Where are we at with Henry Pratt?' Work wasn't really work—we were enjoying ourselves so much." A year or so later Hilles left to build a house for his sister in El Paso, Texas, where he decided to settle permanently. "I sure loved Ed," he says.

In 1953 the Stewart house was completed. It was the first contemporary house on a grand scale I'd ever been in. Phil and Hope Stewart furnished it elegantly and kept it in mint condition. The decorative pool near the front entrance was kept filled and clean, and as you entered you felt as if you were entering a piece of sculpture with glass sides looking west to wide fields. The windows were cleaned once a week.

Stewart house (Herrlin Studio photo)

The dining room was furnished with chairs and a table by the distinguished architect-woodworker, George Nakashima of New Hope, Pennsylvania. Nakashima's designs were simple in the extreme but of such fine wood and workmanship that each piece was in itself a work of art. The Stewarts also had a Nakashima couch in the living room.

In October 1955 the house was chosen by Lake Forest College as one of six to be shown on an architectural tour called The New Architecture. In the ten years after the end of World War II, most residential building was designed to fill the crying need for inexpensive housing quickly. Housing remained in short supply well into the 50s and fine residential architecture was all but unknown. On the North Shore of Chicago there was only a handful of fine houses of contemporary design.

The idea to have an architectural tour of such houses originated with Suzette Morton Zurcher (now Davidson), a member of the Morton family whose name is perpetuated in salt—not to mention the Morton Arboretum, the Morton wing of the Art Institute, and other examples of generosity in and around Chicago. Her exquisite taste and her reputation as an authority on contemporary art were instrumental in convincing the owners to open their houses to the public and allow them to be publicized. Of the six owners, only one insisted on anonymity.

Besides Hope and Phil Stewart's house at 1300 Waukegan Road in Lake Forest, the other North Shore houses were:

Winston Elting house
St. Mary's Road, Libertyville
Architect: Winston Elting

Mildred and Abel E. Fagen house
1851 Old Mill Road, Lake Forest
Architects: George Fred and William Keck

Charles F. Glore house
170 North Mayflower Road, Lake Forest
Architect: Frank Lloyd Wright

Ben Rose house
370 Beech Street, Highland Park
Architect: A. James Speyer

Anonymous Owner
65 South Deere Park Drive, Highland Park
Architect: William F. Deknatel

The tour was a great success, and along with good contemporary design came the realization of many of our wartime dreams. We had washing and drying machines for our clothes; drip dry fabrics that freed us from ironing; we had dishwashers; power lawn mowers; plastics; fluorescent lights; frozen foods; TV and TV dinners; cake mixes; and insecticides like DDT that made outdoor living a pleasant summertime reality. That so many of them turned sour like TV dinners, or lethal like DDT, we were not to know for another decade or two. The decade of the 1950s was the golden age.

In 1954 Ned opened his first Chicago office. It was at 201 North Wells Street. One of his associates, Ed Straka, who joined him in 1956 and who was to stay with him longer than any other associate, tells about that office.

"Ed had entered a competition by the Chicago Association of Commerce and Industry for a renovation of the two top floors of the Corn Products Building. His drawing with a penthouse on top won the competition and an award by *Progressive Architecture,* which featured it in the January 1956 issue. Actually the penthouse was never built, but a deal was struck that allowed him to rent an office at a low rent in exchange for architectural services as other spaces in the building required renovation."

The rental agreement proved satisfactory and new work continued to come in necessitating the addition to the firm of eight or nine architects, some of whom, like Straka, were to become Ned's good friends.

Ned was never good at keeping records or drawings, so there is no reliable list of his work. But the list compiled after his death from many sources indicates that during his five years in the Corn Products

Building, there were over fifty projects, of which all but six were built. The completed projects include twenty-six residences, four churches, and a variety of other buildings such as an apartment complex, a restaurant, a medical facility, and a number of small stores.

Among the residences was the house at 49 Hawthorne Road in Barrington, completed in 1954 for Henry and Maud Beard, both musicians. She is a singer and, until his death in August 1989, he was the most distinguished organ designer in the country. The Beards and Darts, who were to become neighbors, hadn't met until, in Maud's words:

"Ed was building St. Michael's Church in Barrington, and he called Hank for advice about the organ. Ed said he had never built a church before, so Hank came out to Barrington to look things over. It so happened that at just that time we were thinking of buying land and building a house, and when Hank finished talking to Ed he said, 'Maudie, I think we've found our architect.'"

The Beards drove around Barrington looking at sites, and a short while later bought the property on Hawthorne Road, bordering Keene Lake.

The Beard house, Barrington, Illinois (Torkel Korling photo)

149

Interior view of Beard house

"Ed accomplished the impossible," Maudie, who still lives in the house, says. "He had to design a living room big enough to house two pianos, an organ—and all the pipes for the organ—with lots of room for seating, and it still had to be on a human scale. It's a success; people feel comfortable here. They're not overpowered."

Set high on a hill overlooking the lake, the house of glass and common brick has a bird-like grace. It won a Chicago Chapter AIA honor award in 1960.

Another house of this period is Elmer Johnson's in Beverly Hills, a historic section in the southwest corner of Chicago. Johnson, who still lives in the house, says that tours of architectural buffs frequently visit Beverly, "and when I spot them out front lecturing about the house, I frequently invite them to see the interior as well.

"The house is on a small lot, only sixty-three by a hundred and fifty feet, but Ed's solution to the problem was good. He came up with the initial floor plan, and I didn't alter a thing except to ask him to move the

Johnson house in Beverly Hills (Elmer H. Johnson photo)

laundry room upstairs. I felt Ed was a genius as a designer, but not the best engineer in the world."

Like most of Ned's clients, Elmer Johnson got along with him fine. "I chose Ed because I saw the AIA's choice for the ten best buildings all pictured and exhibited in the lobby of Tribune Tower. Three of them appealed to me. So I went to see each one. I liked everything Ed showed me, so I didn't bother with the others."

Dr. Howard Zeiger is another Dart house owner who didn't bother with any others. In 1990 he bought the Norman Miller house at 27 Graymoor Lane in Olympia Fields, Illinois. "It was before my wife and I were married. We were looking at houses and I told her if we saw anything we liked to play it cool—not to show any enthusiasm.

"But from the moment we approached the Dart house I knew it was a work of art. In fact, after ten minutes we decided to buy it. This was

Miller house, Olympia Fields (John MacGaw photo, 1993)

day one of looking at houses and I hadn't even picked up the engagement ring yet.

"This was a decision I am sure we'll never regret."

❧

At about this time, in 1956, after only five years in the house on Spring Creek Road, Ned wanted to move on. He bought land on Oak Knoll Road and built a more formal house, so unlike his first house that I felt it was a betrayal to have abandoned the Spring Creek Road house for it.

It's a split level house, mostly of glass and concrete and has a massive stone chimney dominating one side. It also has a flat roof, and even though many of his most successful buildings have flat roofs, I'm generally prejudiced against them, so I find it hard to be objective.

But it did catch the eye of the critics and home design editors. It was featured in newspapers and in magazines such as *House and Garden* (August 1959) and *Architectural Record* (November 1960) and was given an AIA merit award in 1960.

Dart house, Oak Knoll Road (Herrlin photo, 1956)

In 1957, the year after they moved into their new house, Ned and Wilma received their second child. After the baby's death in 1951 and a stillborn baby four years later, they had put their names on a list for adoption. Since nothing seemed to be imminent, they agreed to spend the Christmas holidays with us at the McCutcheons' island in the Bahamas, which Ned and Wilma had visited and loved.

Elaine Dart and our daughter Mary McCutcheon, were about the same age and were great friends, and Ned needed a break. At just that time the adoption agency called to say it had a baby boy for them. They named him Philip, and Wilma cancelled her Nassau plans but insisted that Ned and Elaine go. They did and they almost didn't make it back.

The first part of our vacation was all we had hoped it would be. The island, called Salt Cay on the charts but Treasure Island in the family, was a wonderful place. It had been in my husband's family for over forty years. Jack's father, born and brought up in rural Indiana, had always longed for the romance of southern seas and an island of his own—preferably an island once frequented by pirates.

In 1916 just before his marriage to Evelyn Shaw, the daughter of poet Frances Wells Shaw and her architect husband, McCutcheon heard of just such an island for sale for $17,500. A man from New Jersey named Abraham Van Winkle had owned it and developed it into a tropical paradise with a main house (the "residency"), two guest houses, servants' cottages and more than a mile of concrete paths through the coconut groves that abounded there. When Van Winkle died, his widow, who apparently never liked the place, wanted to sell. There were few people in those wartime days who wanted to buy an island. My father-in-law was one of those few, and so eager was he that he bought it sight unseen. He took his bride there for their honeymoon in 1917, and the island became the pride and joy of the family for three generations.

The weather was grand when we arrived—warm and sunny. The kids played in the sea, Jack spent most of his time on the beach looking for shells, and Ned relaxed completely. I noticed he was often engrossed in a book on the philosophy of William James. We discussed it and I was struck by how well-read he was and how eloquent when he talked about things he really cared about. For one who probably couldn't even spell philosophy when he was in school, he showed extraordinary comprehension of the subject. He had outstripped me.

We had been at the island a few days when I made plans to go to Nassau for supplies, which we generally did a couple of times a week. Josephas, the caretaker, or Wilfred, the boat man, would sail us over and help haul all the groceries, the ice (we had no electricity), the bottles of sun tan lotion and all the other items we thought we couldn't live without. There was nothing edible on the island except coconuts. The men caught fish occasionally, and for fresh water we used rain water from large cisterns sunk in the ground and covered by wooden tops. We had a couple of flush toilets with overhead water tanks dating back to Van Winkle's day and for bathing we simply used the sea. It was a pleasant, *dolce far niente* way of life, but it did require quite a bit of planning.

Our party numbered seven: Ned and Elaine, Jack and me, and our three children. We also had our little dachshund, Rosie. Josephas Monroe and his wife, Lineth, who did the cooking, were in one of the servant's cottages, and Wilfred Sweeting, who was an expert sailor, was in the other.

Jack and I and our children were in the main house up a slight rise at the highest point above the sea. It stood just back of a sheer cliff with waves constantly pounding against the rocks below—a dramatic setting, especially when the waves were high and the wind was strong.

Ned and Elaine were in one of the guest cottages, the one nearest the sea. It had its own beach and a view of the Atlantic Ocean with nothing between it and Portugal—quite the nicest place for guests to stay.

The day I had planned to go to town (a Thursday) dawned warm and sunny so I postponed my shopping trip. But on Friday, although it was another sunny day, Wilfred said "a rage" was coming and that we'd better wait. Wilfred had a beautiful smile—white teeth, handsome black face, a melodic voice—and he had an instinctive knowledge of the weather and the sea.

It began to blow that evening and I asked Wilfred if this was the rage coming.

"Yes, Madam," he said, smiling and polite as always.

"Wilfred, exactly what is a rage? Is that the same as a hurricane?"

"No, Madam. A hurricane, she be worse. A rage—a rage not as bad as a hurricane, but almost." The wind picked up and blew hard. We closed and bolted all the heavy wooden doors that we usually left wide open night and day. We moved outdoor furniture and hammocks indoors. Ned and Elaine went down to their cottage early to batten down their doors.

The kerosene lamps were lit and flickered behind their glass chimneys as gusts of wind swept under the cracks of the doors. At first it was exciting, and the children laughed at the crashes of thunder they heard above the pounding sea outside. Jack and I thought it best to extinguish the lamps and go to bed, but we didn't sleep much that night. The wind was increasing. The sea was raging harder, and the sounds of rain and thunder were terrifyingly hard to tell apart.

At about two o'clock we heard a fumbling at the door and when we pulled it open, there stood Ned with Elaine wrapped in a blanket in his arms. They were drenched and disheveled, having stumbled up the path around Spanish cove, a small bay between the guest cottages and the main house, where the waves were now sweeping over the rock wall hurling rocks and debris onto the path. The waves had already begun to sweep away the wall, the path, and Ned and Elaine. They got through just in time.

"When a wave crashed through the door and covered the floor with a foot of water before it receded, I knew it was time to leave," he said.

We put them to bed, and the long wait began. It seemed as though the shrieking wind and pounding surf would never let up. Dawn came on Saturday, but it was gray and ugly. It stayed that way all day and finally, twenty-four hours after it had begun, the wind began to abate, but the rain continued and the sea raged on.

We had to stay indoors but there were still books and magazines we hadn't read, and the children had enough things to entertain themselves. Food was running low, however.

By Sunday we began to be hungry. We had a few servings of dry cereal, some sugar, no milk, a few bananas, a jar of bacon drippings and, luckily, an adequate supply of cornmeal. The supply of canned goods was gone. Fishing was out of the question.

We were marooned for five days, and from Sunday to Wednesday we had nothing to eat but a kind of mush Lineth made of cornmeal, water, and bacon drippings, not a candidate for the Cordon Bleu.

A few brave souls ventured outside to inspect the damage but the rain—or possibly it was spray from the surf—and the blowing sand still pounded our faces. We spent most of our time in the living room of the main house. Ned found a long narrow piece of poster board and some pens and poster paints. He drew a long narrow cartoon called Hurricane 1957. In the center were the two little girls, Elaine and Mary, our nine-year-olds, cutting out paper dolls; Pandy, Latin book in hand, was at the desk dutifully studying; I was in a hammock reading; our little boy, John, was teasing the dog; and Jack was far outside battling wind and rain looking for shells.

When Ned showed me the cartoon, I asked where he was. He quickly went to work and in no time handed the cartoon back to me. Along the bottom margin, the entire length of the cardboard, he sketched himself laid out on the floor, an empty bottle of rum by his side, and a scattered deck of cards around him.

We tacked the cartoon up on the wall where it stayed for twenty years, delighting family and guests until it crumbled, and Mrs. McCutcheon died, and the island was sold.

Ned drank a lot but never was drunk as far as I know. He did play with those cards, though, until they were dog-eared, and when I asked him what he was doing, he said he was working out an infallible formula for winning at poker. Fortunately he never found it; if he had, we might have been deprived of some of his best buildings.

By Wednesday morning, five days after the rage had begun, we told Wilfred we wanted to leave. We had plane reservations, the kids had to get back to school, and the men had to get back to work.

The chief difficulty was getting from the lagoon where the boat was anchored through the cut into the open sea that lay between us and Nassau harbor, seven miles away. The cut was a passage about sixty feet long and fourteen wide which Van Winkle had sawn through the soft coral rock. The powerful waves smashing into the cut could easily smash the small sailboat to smithereens—or engulf it, or both—if Wilfred did not time his entry into the cut just right. Anyone hurled against the sharp rocks was not likely to reach a ripe old age.

"What do you think, Wilfred? Can we make it?"

"Madam," he said, all smiles. "We can try." When pressed he admitted he had never before taken a boat through the cut in such heavy seas.

"You can try doing what Mrs. Marquand did," he suggested.

Mrs. Marquand was the wife of John Marquand, the author, who for many years rented the island during the early winter as a place to write in peace and have his family around him at the same time.

Adelaide Marquand, it seems, had wanted to go to Nassau one day in rough weather. When Wilfred pointed out the height of the waves and the possibility of foundering, she instructed him to "pour oil on troubled waters," assuring him that it was a direction straight from the Bible. It turned out there was no oil on the island, only a partly full ten gallon tin of kerosene. She told Wilfred to go out on the rocks and pour the kerosene on the waves.

"And then what happened, Wilfred?" we asked.

"Oh Madam, Oh Boss," he laughed his rapturous laugh, "it were a waste of good kerosene." Mrs. Marquand postponed her trip.

We debated the question and finally decided to chance it. We all put on slickers and life jackets. We went below in the tiny cabin. The sails remained furled and the engine, after several tries, finally agreed to start.

Wilfred approached the cut, watched the foaming seas ahead and at the right moment revved up that recalcitrant motor to full speed. He usually went straight through that cut with only inches to spare, never scraping the sides. This time we were dashed against one side and then the other and back again. We were thrown up, our heads hitting the hatch, and then flung down on the floor. The motor sputtered. Wilfred pushed the throttle. A wave completely washed over us. The motor caught and we kept going.

We were through the cut, but another wave hit us. And another. Water began to pour into the cabin. We were thrown about, tangled, wet, scared, and silent—even the dog and the children. The cracking sounds of the mast and sides of the boat were terrifying. I guess we were all praying.

It took almost two hours of battling the sea to reach Nassau harbor. When we got there we couldn't believe it. Completely protected on two sides, the harbor was as still as a pond. The only evidence of the storm was the number of battered boats beginning to come in for repairs. We hadn't had much of a holiday, but at least we were alive.

Soon after we got back home Jack and I began seriously to talk of building our own house. We had been living in an old frame house (no longer standing) that my mother-in-law owned at 194 Illinois Road across from St. Mary's Church in Lake Forest.

We had moved there in 1947 when we were expecting our second child and when housing was still short, but we considered it a stopgap. It represented everything I thought a house shouldn't be. For starters it had two maids' rooms and a bath off the kitchen and no maids in sight. It was also drafty, flaky of plaster, and murder on the back and legs if you were bringing up a family of children, dogs, a cat or two, and if you wanted some semblance of order.

So it was with eager anticipation that we began formal talks with Ned. It was my first visit to his office in the Corn Products Building on Wells Street. I remember the front desk and the bustle in the drafting room, where several men were at work.

We had a list of requirements, which we went over, along with an outline of our budget. A week or so later, Ned called us in to see his first drawing. It was a terrible disappointment—a sort of squared off building, split level, with a flat roof. We rejected it. So the matter was closed until he could come up with something more acceptable for us. I was tired of climbing stairs. I wanted a one-story house. We did not like the sterile look of box houses. We wanted a pitched roof.

A few days later Ned called to say he was nearby and had an idea. He stopped by the house, pulled out a stub of a pencil, and on the back of an envelope sketched the perfect house for us. He had in his mind not only the floor plan, but the total concept of the structure.

From then on the plans for the house went smoothly except for one or two owner-architect arguments. Ned had placed the bathtubs under windows, which Jack, who had lived through enough Northern Illinois winters to know, insisted he change, and I battled over the open area between kitchen and dining area. I wanted it closed off with a pass through. We were right on both counts. We also demurred at the cathedral ceiling and the generous spaciousness of the living room, but Ned insisted. He was right.

We had planned the house for a lot we had tentatively bought near the lake, but when that fell through and we bought land from Ann and Larry Carton on West Laurel Avenue, there was no problem. Except for the front driveway, the design fit into the new setting beautifully. We broke ground in August 1957, and moved in December 1958.

McCutcheon house in Lake Forest, Illinois

Interior views of McCutcheon house

(Barbara Wood-Prince photo)

(Jana Brinton photo)

There was only one major problem with the house. As in so many of Ned's houses, it was difficult to know where the front door was. Almost everyone came to the back door—guests dressed up for a dinner party as well as the garbage man. It was disconcerting, but we finally rectified the error twenty-five years later by tearing out the original driveway and front walk and putting in a new driveway that brought you unerringly to the front door.

We lived in the house for thirty-three years and except for the front entrance and some plumbing problems we had early on, I cannot imagine a more satisfactory house to have lived in. Ed Straka came to the house in September 1989 and said, "I remember so well working on this house. The kind of individual, painstaking, careful work we did on a house like this would have been impossible in a big office."

He pointed to a heavy beam separating the space between the living and dining areas. "You see that beam there? We worked days on that beam. We wanted it to be in proportion. I thought it might be too heavy, but I see it came out just right."

Unfortunately in 1992 we had to sell the house. Jack and I bought 200 acres of land with an old cabin on it in Saluda, North Carolina, in 1979. We loved the place and the climate, and after Jack retired from the *Chicago Tribune,* we decided to build a substantial house in North Carolina and forego the Lake Forest house. We sold it in January and by May it was demolished to make way for a house twice its size.

But when we built it, an outcome like that was the last thing we could have imagined. The world then lay before us "like a land of dreams, so various, so beautiful, so new."

During that same year, 1958, Ned designed three other houses, two churches, and several additions, all of which were completed. One of the churches won two awards and was featured in any number of newspapers and architectural journals—partly, I'm sure, because it's so photogenic. The silhouette of its curved roof line sweeping upward like praying hands makes a marvelous picture.

It is St. Augustine's Church in Gary, Indiana, an Episcopal church with an African-American congregation. The simplicity of the structure

St. Augustine's Church, Gary, Indiana

and the use of simple materials—plain wood and concrete—appealed to people eager to break away from traditional styles, even in churches. During his career Ned was to design thirty churches, twenty-six of which were built.

Soon after we built our house, a woman named Mary Daley joined the Dart office force. She became so much a part of things that it's impossible to discuss Ned's work without mentioning her. I remember the first time I heard of her.

I was talking to Ned about typewriters—he had just bought a new IBM Executive typewriter, and I warned him that it was difficult to correct mistakes on that model.

"That's no problem," Ned said, "Mary Daley never makes mistakes." Mary Daley was twenty-eight when she started working for him. She had been working elsewhere since she was eighteen.

"I had to go to work right after high school," she says. "My mother was sick and we needed the money." Her mother died soon thereafter, and in addition to a full-time job and secretarial classes at night, Mary Daley had to take over the housework which included cooking for her father and looking after her twelve-year-old brother. She eventually got her secretarial degree and began working at various offices including an engineering outfit in Chicago's loop. "A crazy place to work," she says. "I had to get out of there or go crazy too."

It happened that at about that time Ned began working with that same firm of engineers. Mary Daley often had to call Ned's office and established a phone friendship with his secretary, Marge.

"I guess I must have told her that I planned to leave my job," Mary Daley says, "and one day Marge called to say she was getting married and did I want her job. I told her, no, I didn't want any connection with the job I was leaving. Then I said to myself, 'Maybe I'd like to work for an architect,' so she and I and Ed had lunch together and that did it. I stayed with him twelve years.

"In 1959 only a couple of months after I began, we moved from North Wells Street to the Material Services Building at 130 North Franklin. We needed more space."

Ed Straka, who had been with the firm three years, remembers it well. "Every time we moved, we did it ourselves. We rented a truck over the weekend and Ed and I and a couple of others hauled out the files and transported them to the new office. Actually that office at 130 North Franklin wasn't very satisfactory, but we stayed there four years anyhow. We were too busy to move. We were building quite a few churches at that time."

Some of the churches were successful, some weren't, and some never got off the ground. The Presbyterian Church in Lansing, Illinois, was one of the successful ones. Made of Ned's favorite common brick, it rises stark and straight against the sky, making a striking subject for photographers. It received a lot of publicity and two awards. Ned was becoming known as a church architect.

Another church, St. Augustine's Episcopal Church in Benton Harbor, Michigan, built in 1962, was less successful. It has a strange roof resembling the handles of a beverage carton. Father Michael Komechak, head of the fine arts department of Illinois Benedictine College and a frequent lecturer on Dart's church architecture, says that when he went to

Lansing Presbyterian Church (Hedrich-Blessing photo/Chicago Historical Society Collection)

Benton Harbor to photograph the church, "The first person I asked for directions said, 'Oh, you mean the six-pack church.'" Komechak goes on to explain that Ned put the handle on to protect the skylight. "It's not one of Dart's best churches."

It was soon after Ned moved to the Franklin Street office that he met Richard Pepper, a meeting that proved to be a turning point in his career. It started with a four-story parking garage in Chicago at Wabash Avenue and Adams Street that Ned had designed in 1959. Pepper Construction Co. was the low bidder and got the job. Dick Pepper, the son of the founder of the company, was in charge and he and Ned, who was ten years older, hit it off immediately. It turned out that the Peppers, who had five children, lived in Barrington too, and the two families quickly developed a friendship that lasted beyond Ned's death.

Realizing how harmoniously they worked together, they began to recommend each other. Besides working together, they also vacationed together.

"Ed always kept himself in good physical shape," Pepper recalls. "He liked boating and so did I. We first went houseboating together and then we bought a boat together." This boat, which was large enough to cruise the Caribbean, became one of the joys of Ned's life. He and Wilma spent all of their vacations on it until he died.

"It was a great extravagance," Wilma says, "but it was his dream to own a boat. I was all for this venture. He was under so much stress, and I'm grateful that we were able to take off occasionally for a weekend alone or for longer periods with close friends like the Peppers or the Beards. This may be stretching it a bit but I think that Ed, having been a pilot during the war, loved being the captain. He loved being in command of his ship."

As business grew Ned looked for a more congenial office location and he found it in 1962.

"It was an old house at 21 East Superior Street," Mary Daley says. "It was a good place. Everyone was happy in that office. Of course, we were happy in all of Ed's offices. It was fun working there. We were a team—no jealousy, no politics—just good people working together."

Ed Straka says much the same thing. "The move to Superior Street made a good thing better. It was a nice area with a parking lot behind the building, and having the office in an old house was unique. Ed hoped to buy that building ultimately. He never wanted to be in a regular office building downtown."

It's part of the tragedy that befell Ned that he didn't buy the old house at 21 East Superior Street. It's still standing as I write this, but it looks empty and abandoned.

During the summer of 1962 our daughter, Pandy, whose real name is Anne Dart McCutcheon, was approaching senior year at Radcliffe, and planning to go to architectural school. She applied to Ned for a summer job.

When our children were little they used to address Ned as "big, strong, handsome Uncle Ned." Pandy would sometimes throw in a few extra adjectives like "brilliant, important, and rich Uncle Ned" which always amused him, especially the final adjective. He gave her the job.

"I remember what a good time I had there that summer in the office on Superior Street," she says. "It was a walk-up to the second floor and when you got there it was beautiful—intimately scaled. Everybody was happy. I worked with Mary Daley and really liked her.

"There were several draftsmen there but I didn't get to know them very well. We were busy and there was no chewing the fat. But that didn't mean we didn't have fun or laugh a lot.

"One day I transferred a call to one of the draftsmen and I heard him call out to Uncle Ned, 'Hey, Ed. Mrs. N is on the phone again and she's using ugly four-letter words. Words like r-a-i-n and r-o-o-f and l-e-a-k.'"

Besides answering the phone Pandy was given filing and typing to do. "I used to type specs and would take it upon myself to correct spelling and other errors. Once there were the words 'concrete to be screeded,' so I changed it to 'screened.' 'Screeded' was right, of course, and Uncle Ned was upset. 'Just type it the way it is,' he said. 'Don't use your brain.'"

Pandy went on to Harvard and became a practicing architect in 1970. She is now married to Ron Lewis, a lawyer, and has her own architectural firm in Washington, D.C. (McCartney and Lewis). Our son, John McCutcheon III, doubtless influenced by his uncle, also became an architect as well as a structural engineer and is married to still another architect, June Uhlman.

Ned was at 21 East Superior from 1961-1965, the years of some of his best work. "We had time to do things right," Ed Straka says. Among buildings of this period were the United Parcel Service Building at 1400 South Jefferson Street in Chicago; the Holy Apostles Greek Orthodox Church in Westchester, Illinois; and his own last house, completed in 1965, at 66 Dundee Lane in Barrington, all of which won AIA awards.

Ned had begun to think of building another house for his family a couple of years before. This time he bought ten acres of rolling land in Barrington Hills overlooking Keene Lake, next door to the Beards on one side and not far from the Peppers on the other. There was once an old barn on the place, and since the foundations were still strong, Ned used them for his foundations as well as for his theme. The house which is, as usual, of common brick, rises to an extravagant height with an intricate system of criss-crossing beams inside. There are five or six levels reached by a dizzying series of steps—all of it majestic to look at, though not very practical to heat or clean. But since all of the living quarters—kitchen, dining room, living room, study, three bedrooms and two baths—are on

Dart house in Barrington (Warren Meyer photo)

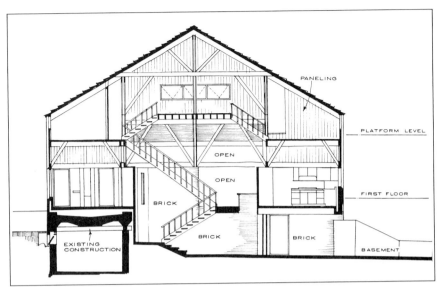

Cross section of Dart house

Dart house, 66 Dundee Lane, Barrington, Illinois
(Hedrich-Blessing photo/Chicago Historical Society Collection)

Interior of Dart house (Hedrich-Blessing photo/Chicago Historical Society Collection)

one level, it's convenient withal. A guest room and bath are downstairs with a studio-living room that opens to a path leading to a swimming pool.

"Yes, it's extravagant," he told me when he saw how awestruck I was. But he wanted it that way. He also wanted to get into big time architecture. "I'm tired of houses," he said to me. "I want to do big buildings."

"Ed was impatient," Ed Straka says. "We got nothing but relatively small jobs in our office. People would come to Ed and get him to design their houses, but when they wanted to design an office building or a factory they'd go to some big firm.

"Perkins and Will approached Ed to go in with them, but he turned them down. All the architects in town knew he was one of the great designers and any one of the big offices would have been glad to get him, but he wouldn't go."

At least not until he was approached by Loebl Schlossman and Bennett in 1965. "I don't know what changed his mind," Straka says. "Maybe he knew he didn't have much time left. Nothing would be the same for any of us after that."

It was Jerrold Loebl who approached Ned. Loebl's partners were Norman Schlossman and Richard Bennett. In 1965, with an office at 333 North Michigan Avenue, the firm was clearly in the forefront nationally as well as locally.

Jerry Loebl (1897-1978) and Norm Schlossman (1901-1990), both Chicagoans, had known each other as architecture students at Armour Institute (now Illinois Institute of Technology) where they had been graduated in 1921. In 1925 they opened an office together at 612 North Michigan Avenue. They weathered the depression and by the end of World War II they were ready for the enormous building boom that followed. In 1949 the firm became Loebl Schlossman and Bennett.

Richard Bennett, born in 1907 in Pennsylvania and a graduate of Harvard's architectural school, was chairman of the department of architecture at Yale when Ned entered. In addition to his academic success, Bennett's architectural achievements are legendary. He was the chief designer for Park Forest, the new town south of Chicago, which came to be recognized as the prototype for new town developments and suburban shopping centers all over the world. He went on to complete any number of successful projects including Old Orchard Shopping Center (1955); Oakbrook Shopping Center (1961); Congregation Solel in Highland Park, Illinois (1962); Chicago Loop Synagogue (1963); Greenwood Mall in Greenwood, Indiana (1964); Gateway Shopping Center in Lincoln, Nebraska (1965); River Oaks Shopping Center in Calumet City, Illinois (1966); and Hawthorn Center in Vernon Hills, Illinois (1973).

In 1965 the firm was expanding rapidly, and it was at just that moment that Ned was ripe for the big time. His admiration for Richard Bennett, with whom he had kept in touch since Yale, also undoubtedly influenced him. They offered him a partnership and he accepted.

"We would have made it big on our own," Ed Straka says. "If only Ed had waited, but it would have taken time and Ed wanted it now."

"Actually we were at a crossroads," Mary Daley says. "We had struggled so—a hand to mouth existence—and at just that time the work was increasing. The staff couldn't handle it, and Ed had to go one way or the other. Should he hire more draftsmen and get bigger, or stay small? And along came Jerry Loebl."

"It was a tremendous decision," Wilma says. "Should he continue on his own or join a larger firm? We talked about it a lot—reviewed the pros and cons, but the decision had to be his own. I knew he wanted to do bigger buildings and hated all the book work and details of running an office. He wanted to create without the hassle of meeting the payroll for a larger staff. I wasn't much help in his decision, but he knew that whatever he chose to do I was one hundred percent behind him." He chose to join the firm which would be called Loebl Schlossman Bennett and Dart.

"It was not a happy time," Mary Daley says. "Ed didn't coax any of us to go over with him and some of the staff felt left out. The real problem was money. Loebl Schlossman and Bennett didn't want to pay any more than they had to, and the bald fact is that they didn't want Ed's whole office force. In the end no one moved over except Ed Straka's brother, Paul, who was just out of school and whose salary was low, and me. And I had to take a cut from $175 to $145 a week. Ed Straka and one other architect stayed on in the old office to finish up a few small jobs and the others went elsewhere."

Ed Straka subsequently opened his own office in his home in Riverside, Illinois. Paul Straka stayed with Ned only about a year before opening his own office devoted largely to religious buildings. Mary Daley stayed with Ned six more years.

In recounting those years she says, "The Loebl office at 333 North Michigan was on the twenty-fourth floor. Soon after Ed got there, he began redesigning it. He used common brick, put in a window between the hall and the reception area, and built a beautiful reception desk. The effect was clean and light. We had yellow walls, parquet floors and a built-in couch. The desk was gorgeous—free form with walnut sides and a black formica top. It wasn't very convenient, but that didn't matter because it was so good looking."

There is considerable controversy about Ned's decision to join Loebl. Some critics say that immediately after he did so, his work lost the human touch, that it reflected the brash, big-city approach.

"That's not so," says Michael Komechak who was in close touch with Ned from 1965 on. "The architectural community was against Dart's joining a big firm. No one applauded the move, but look at the facts. Some of the best work he did was after 1965."

Looking at the press clippings of those years, one must agree. He was frequently being featured in the Chicago newspapers—in the *Daily News,* the *Tribune* and the *Sun Times*—and in architectural journals such as *Progressive Architecture* and *Inland Architect,* not to mention the trade journals and church magazines. He also wrote a number of eloquent articles on the state of architecture that would have astonished his old teachers in Virginia who had held out so little hope for him. The number of awards he won would also have astonished them. Altogether there were more than thirty, eighteen of which were from the AIA.

"The reason he won so many AIA awards," Ed Straka says, "is that he was one of the few who was able to understand Mies van der Rohe and the international school without simply turning out sterile boxes as most of the others at that time did. In the same way he was influenced by Frank Lloyd Wright but never copied him. His architecture, in short, was his own."

In 1967 Ned was made a fellow of the AIA. Among the letters recommending him was one from a professor of theology at the University of Chicago, Joseph Sittler, which ended:

> Edward Dart listens and what he hears and sees and senses he manages with exquisite sensibility to translate into form and structure and texture. And he does this without the employment of gimmicks, cosmetic or meaningless rhetoric.

ॐ

Beginning in 1966 and finishing in 1970 Ned created what is generally considered his best work, St. Procopius Abbey in Lisle, Illinois.

St. Procopius Abbey was founded in Chicago in 1885 in the Pilsen neighborhood on 18th Street. Largely serving Slavic immigrants, it grew until it consisted not only of the monastery, but also a high school, a college, and a seminary. In 1901 the monks bought a farm in the then sparsely populated area of Lisle, thirty miles west of Chicago. By 1915 all four operations were moved to Lisle and housed in one large building now called Benedictine Hall.

St. Procopius continued to grow, and by 1965 it was clear that the monks needed a separate monastery. The abbot, Daniel Kucera, turned the job of finding an architect over to Michael Komechak, who had been at St. Procopius since his freshmen year in high school and who had become a monk in 1955.

"I had two committees of five monks each, and I interviewed about a hundred people," Komechak says. "I started the hunt in June 1965, and I took almost a year to complete it. We narrowed the field down to four architects and invited them out to Lisle to see the site and talk to the monks. We thought Dart was the best architect for the project. On Valentine's Day, 1966, the contract was signed and three months later the design for the organ by Hank Beard was begun."

Ned's design was completed in 1967 and construction began early in 1968. Long before it was finished the monastery began to attract attention. Photographers love a photogenic subject and St. Procopius Abbey is photogenic. Rising clean and unadorned with its angular shape silhouetted against the sky, it offers a dramatic contrast to its busy surroundings.

The monks moved in in June 1970, and inside the atmosphere is of serenity. No ornamentation mars the purity of design, and yet there is a feeling of warmth and humanness at every turn.

More than a score of articles on St. Procopius appeared within a couple of years of its completion, all favorable. Then came the awards. The Chicago chapter of the AIA gave it the Distinguished Building award in 1971, and in 1973 it won the AIA's National Honor Award. The following year the Brick and Tile Institute issued a handsome color brochure on the abbey and gave it its award. It would be gratifying to report that the building was an unqualified success, which it is from a

St. Procopius Abbey (Philip A. Turner photo)

design standpoint, but for basic functioning it has had a few problems.

The original roof had to be replaced after only five years. It was a tern roof of a zinc alloy called Titanoloy, which simply disintegrated. Ned, the Abbey, and Pepper Construction Co. shared the cost of replacing it with a new stainless steel roof in 1975.

Another problem arose from the Chicago common brick Ned used in almost every building he built. It turns out that this is not a satisfactory material over a long period of time. The brick flakes and ultimately crumbles, but apparently it does so faster on some buildings than on others. The brick on our house, built in 1958, only began to show signs of deterioration thirty years later. The brick at St. Procopius began flaking in 1985 after barely fifteen years. The Abbey has spent more than $80,000 having the worst bricks replaced by drilling out the mortar, removing the old brick, and replacing it. Komechak is optimistic that a silicone treatment may hold the problem in check.

St. Procopius is not the first building that required major repair work. Restoration architect John Vinci told me that he was called in to repair the roof on the Chicago Theological Seminary Faculty Housing Complex, another AIA award-winning project, which Ned completed in 1962.

"The cause," Vinci says, "was partly deteriorating brick and partly inadequate flashing."

Faculty Housing, Chicago Theological Seminary

But for the most part Ned's work during the early years at Loebl Schlossman Bennett and Dart was given high marks. Commissions for new buildings and awards came thick and fast. Altogether he worked on forty-five projects while he was a partner there, all but four completed and none of them insignificant. Among the completed projects were the Samsonite Corporation office building in Denver, Colorado; Pick Staiger Concert Hall, Norris University Center and Nathaniel Leverone Hall, all at Northwestern University in Evanston; the service school and barracks at Great Lakes Naval Training Center; six churches; and a variety of other buildings including several schools, medical facilities, and offices.

If the people who actually use these buildings were canvassed to discover which among them worked the best or was the most appreciated, the Pick-Staiger Concert Hall at Northwestern would be among the top runners—almost certainly the top. The staff working in the building is almost reverential as they speak of the place. "It makes me feel good just to be here," said a young woman working in the office when I visited recently.

People still talk of the distinguished musician, John Paynter ("the most demanding chairman of any department Northwestern ever had"), who stopped his first rehearsal in the hall to say that he had been in practically every great music hall in the world and "this one here at Northwestern is the greatest." Every musician and music lover I talked to agreed. A concert pianist said to me, "After playing in the Pick-Staiger, it spoils you for anywhere else."

Why? The music sounds better—it's as simple and as complex as that. "It's gorgeous," says Nancy Graham, John Paynter's department assistant. "The sound is beautiful and so is the sight. As you come up the hill, you see the Pick-Staiger and you want to stop and look at it, and once inside you can look out at the lake and the Chicago Skyline. It's bright and beautiful."

Constructed primarily of precast concrete and glass, the building has 1,003 seats, all of which have an unobstructed view of the stage. In other words, every seat is equally good for viewing and hearing. There are no posts or balcony overhangs, which in part accounts for the crystal-like sound. In addition there are thirty plastic dish-shaped panels over the

Entrance to Pick-Staiger Concert Hall, Northwestern University (Claude Peck photo)

Pick-Staiger Concert Hall stage showing plastic panels (Claude Peck photo)

Photo showing unobstructed view of the stage,
Pick-Staiger Concert Hall (Claude Peck photo)

stage and acoustical drapery which can be adjusted to meet the particular requirements of each performance.

Ground was broken in 1966, but the building was not opened until October 1975—just a few weeks too late for Ned to be there. He loved music.

But if it sounds as if Ned's architecture was universally admired, I have given the wrong impression. There were lots of people who were less than complimentary. When we were planning our house in Lake Forest, our neighbor Ann Carton, who sold us the land and who liked Dart architecture, told me that another neighbor was overheard remarking, "Now we're going to have a Dart hot-dog stand built nearby."

Among the few newspaper clippings Ned saved was a handwritten polemic on Dart architecture. It was scribbled in the margin of a 1965 article on the subject of suburban architecture in which several architects, including Ned, are quoted. The anonymous author of the handwritten critique circled certain adjectives in the article, *banal, idiotic, senseless, absurd, insane,* and wrote, "All this applies to the obscene warehouse you built last year in Glencoe. Shame on you ... I want you to know it's the talk of the North Shore, If I were you I would not admit it to anyone."

There's an old saying that goes, "When they start attacking you, you know you are making progress." If that is so, Ned was soon to make real progress.

In July 1970 the biggest project he was ever to tackle was announced. It was to design a mixed-use development on North Michigan Avenue across from the Old Water Tower, one of the few buildings to survive the great Chicago fire of 1871. Called at first Water Tower Plaza (later Water Tower Place), the building project and its site were the most desirable in Chicago at that time.

Ned tackled the project eagerly. "The greatest, most exciting project I've been privileged to do," he is quoted as saying in the *Chicago Tribune* (November 20, 1971). The building, the first of its kind, was to be a city in itself, a 3,100,000 square-foot vertical shopping center with a hotel, apartments, offices, restaurants, a theater, a parking garage, and shops and stores galore—all under one roof, seventy-four stories high. It would ultimately cost $160 million.

What he didn't anticipate was the complexity of a project this size, the complexity of trying to satisfy two owners and the various other individuals and requirements involved. He never spoke to me at length about it, but as the project took shape, he was clearly disappointed that it had become, in his words, a committee project. He was particularly disappointed by the choice of grey Georgian marble for the exterior instead of the less glitzy Texas granite he had specified. The clients (Mafco, Inc., a subsidiary of Marshall Field & Co., and Urban Investment and Development Co., headed by Philip Klutznick) insisted on marble as more appropriate for the air of luxury and prestige they wanted to achieve. Marshall Field's, Lord and Taylor, and the Ritz-Carlton Hotel would be the principal tenants.

There were endless other disagreements and compromises along with lots of promotional publicity. What is astonishing, in view of the architectural horrors that were, and still are, being perpetrated in Chicago, is how much adverse criticism Water Tower Place generated even before it got off the ground. In 1971 the first designs were out and from that moment on, the critics had a heyday.

Except for architect Harry Weese and Rob Cuscaden, of the *Chicago Sun-Times,* I can discover no architects or critics who had a kind word to say about it. Weese said in a letter to Ned that he liked the design and that "the Magnificent Mile will be even more so." Cuscaden's feeling in 1973 was that the building could "hold its own with any of its big brothers around town." But by the time the rest of the pack went out for the kill, he joined them and described it as "men's room modern." Most critics are like little children. They seem to rely on the opinion of the gang, and then they go for it, or against it, as the case may be. Luckily critics (of art, architecture, literature, anything) have had little or no lasting influence over the ages.

Among the other critics whose derogatory criticisms have had no effect whatsoever on the success of the building was the then editor of *Inland Architect,* Nory Miller, in the January-February 1974 issue of *Architectural Forum.* She refers to Water Tower Place as a beast and says "it will be no inspiring silhouette on Chicago's skyline. The design is an awkward shapeless montage. An arbitrary splicing from the cutting room floor." Her implication is that "the faceless sterility of the exterior" and "the machine age interpretation of the Villa Borghese" on the interior will be a disaster.

In the July 1977 issue of *Chicago* magazine, Alice Weil quotes some of the criticism of Water Tower Place both before and after it was completed. In her words:

> Paul Goldberger, critic for the *New York Times,* labeled the marble facade "dreary and pretentious."
>
> Critic M. W. Newman, writing in the Chicago-based *Inland Architect,* called Water Tower Place "the 'everything' building that provides Michigan Avenue with everything but architectural or urban grace."...
>
> And urban historian Carl Condit has referred to Water Tower Place as "a deplorable building."

Water Tower Place (Joseph J. Lucas photo, 1993)

Elevator in Water Tower Place (Ann Duncan photo, 1993)

It was the late Paul Gapp in the November 30, 1975, *Chicago Tribune* whose attack is the most unrelenting. Gapp, a Pulitzer prize winner, had generally praised Ned's work, and in this article mentions "a legacy of many excellent churches, residences, and other buildings which brought him awards. For these he will be remembered."

But in describing Water Tower Place he pulls out all the stops. Under the headline "A marble block mars the Mile's magnificence," he refers to Water Tower Place as a flop and says, "it always will be one of Chicago's most prominent architectural failures of the late 20th Century."

He embellishes this by saying that the building "says nothing of itself but manages to present embarrassingly ugly facades at the same time. Water Tower Place is a dowdy young millionairess with warts on her nose." Of the tower he says, "It is difficult to imagine how it could have been done more badly." The exterior, he adds, has "a soiled, cobwebby look" whose "overall visual impact is a cold, sepulchral ugliness."

Donald Hackl, who worked with Ned on Water Tower and who is today head of the firm (now Loebl Schlossman and Hackl), calls such criticism petty in the 1977 article in *Chicago* magazine by Alice Weil. He explains that a building of that size has to be economically viable and that it should be judged by the benefits that accrue from it, which as it turned out have been many. Besides being a success economically and visually, it is like a magnet to out of town visitors who almost always put it high on their sight-seeing lists. In his 1990 assessment (*The Sky's the Limit / A Century of Chicago Skyscrapers*), John Zukowsky of The Art Institute of Chicago refers to Water Tower Place as a "spectacular multiuse project" that attracts over twenty million visitors a year.

I liked it from the beginning and still do. I particularly like (in spite of Ned) the two tones of beautiful grey marble on the exterior, and I like the dramatic interior with its glorious live gardens cascading down the sides of the escalators, and I like the gorgeous many-faceted glass elevator. The whole building is elegant.

At the same time Ned was trying to create something good in spite of the obstacles put in his path, he received still another important commission. It was to design the King Faisal Cancer Research and Treatment Center (now called the Cancer Treatment Institute) in Riyadh, Saudi

Arabia. The commission came about through Dick Pepper.

"We got the Arab job through American Hospital Supply, for whom I had done work," Pepper says. "The Arabs had hired a British firm to design the King Faisal Hospital, but when the British shipped arms to Israel, the Arabs cut them off. Ed and I went to Geneva, Switzerland, together and met the Arab representatives, including a doctor. They needed a cyclotron. Ed hadn't any idea what that was, so he went to Stanford University to find out. He studied hard and in three weeks he was ready. That was in 1974."

In the meanwhile Pepper told the Arabs that there were Jewish partners in Ned's firm. "They accepted that," he says. "Ed made several trips to Saudi Arabia and in 1975 the design was complete. We never had to change a thing; we built it exactly as Ed designed it."

During all this time of hectic traveling and designing, Ned was painting. He had taken up water colors in 1973 and was growing more enthusiastic about his painting than about his career. Whenever we went to his house he would insist that we look at the pictures he had completed, most of them tacked up on the walls. In two years he completed a substantial body of work. In the spring of 1975 the Tavern Club at 333 North Michigan Avenue (the same building where his office was) had an exhibit of his work; more than 100 paintings were displayed.

That was the year Ned was going at the highest speed he had ever traveled. Water Tower Place was under construction; he was flying to Saudi Arabia and elsewhere; he was working on several buildings, among them a church, St. John of the Cross in Western Springs, Illinois, that was to win for him a posthumous AIA award in 1978—and he was painting, painting.

July 4 fell on a Friday in 1975. It was a long weekend and for once Ned relaxed with his family and friends. In the middle of the night on Sunday, or early Monday, July 7, Wilma heard him stirring in the bed next to her. "I didn't think anything of it," she says. "He often got up in the middle of the night and went downstairs to paint. In fact that's when he did most of his work. But a little later I awoke and heard him mumbling."

To her horror she found that he had fallen on the floor and was unconscious. Elaine called us that morning to say he had had a stroke and had been taken to Sherman Hospital in nearby Elgin.

I called Elaine or Wilma several times that day and the next, and always the report I got was the same. Though he had not regained consciousness, he was exceptionally strong and all his vital signs were good. There was, according to the hospital, no cause for alarm.

At 7:30 in the morning on Wednesday, July 9, Elaine called and said, "Aunt Susan, the hospital just called and said that Dad has just minutes to live."

I was in shock but I moved fast and without thinking. I got in my car and raced to Elgin. Jack meanwhile called New Orleans. Mother and Dad, and Ninette were not at home when he called. They had gone to Mass to pray for Ned.

When I got to the Sherman Hospital, I raced to the desk and said I was Edward Dart's sister and had to see him.

They tried to prevent me. Hospital personnel have a strange aversion to death. They can't face it and don't like to admit it happened. I insisted until they said, "Your brother has passed away."

"You mean he died," I said and they said, "He passed away."

They nevertheless took me to the cubicle in intensive care where he was, and I put my hand on his shoulder. How thin it was. He was still warm. His arms were out of the sheets and his head was to one side. He had a smile on his face.

"Oh, Ned," I said aloud, and I knew he could still hear me. "You are gone from us now but you are with Grand-mère and Grand-père and Roger. And you're with Bill Senhauser and Bobo Harbison," My tears wet the hospital gown he was dressed in.

I left soon and found Wilma and Elaine standing alone in the hospital chapel. They had gotten there too late too. He had died five minutes after Elaine called me.

They were quiet. Wilma had on a summer dress and a white sweater. She looked calm and beautiful and has never ceased in all these years to be the courageous person she was at that moment. Bless her.

Why did Ned die so young? He was just fifty-three. The medical report called it an embolism, and Dick Pepper, who saw him almost daily, agrees. "Ed died from a clot," he says. "Sure, he was going at high speed and he smoked and drank, but that was not the cause. He was in good physical condition—he exercised. The explanation is simply what the doctors say, an embolism."

Others who knew him disagree. It was no secret that he was unhappy over the way Water Tower Place was shaping up—unhappy when he found he couldn't make the architectural decisions alone. Architect Stanley Tigerman, who was forty-four at the time, tells about lunching with Ned at the Tavern Club a week before he died. That was just when the final decision was about to be made on what material would be put on the outside of Water Tower Place—granite or marble.

"We were to lunch alone but Jerry Loebl joined us. We were glad to have him. Jerry was nice but it was a sad time. Ed pleaded with Jerry not to let the clients have their way and put that wash room marble on the outside of Water Tower, and Jerry joked and cajoled. But he was going to do it their way, and he did. It broke Ed's heart. If anyone ever died of a broken heart it was Ed."

Almost all the architects who knew Ned think that he should have stayed on his own and not gotten involved in the politics of big deals. "He was caught in the big-business trap," Ed Straka says. "His latest work was devoid of the human touch. I think that if he had lived he would not have participated much longer—not in what is called architecture today, anyhow.

"Architecture today is inhuman. It is out of scale and there is no realization of what it is supposed to accomplish. We'll have a few old monuments and everything else will be destroyed. Our profession is really twisted."

Stanley Tigerman says much the same thing. "Ed was a great person—a fine architect until he made that one big mistake—joining Loebl. Everything he did that was small and on a human scale was good. It was honest.

"But he saw others—Bruce Graham and the like—in big offices and he wanted to do big things too. In the end he knew it was a mistake. He knew that he was no longer making a lot of the decisions—the big decisions."

Michael Komechak, on the other hand, thinks that Ned was where he wanted to be. "He had just been made president of the firm and he would have reformed the office and gone on to even greater things. He would never have given up architecture."

Wilma agrees. "I lived with him and he was happy with the situation until Water Tower Place. He designed some very fine buildings during those years. Unfortunately his experience with Water Tower—with politicians and big real estate developers who had commercial success as the only objective—this crucified him. He was miserable during most of the process, but he would never have given up architecture. He probably would have scaled down his practice, and he certainly would never again have accepted a commission that was not completely within his control, but I don't think he could have survived without creating buildings. He loved painting and wanted to devote more time to it, but it could never have replaced his number one love, architecture."

Ned was buried on Friday, July 11, 1975, in the columbarium of St. Michael's Church, the one he designed in Barrington. Among the flowers was an arrangement of tropical foliage sent by some of his World War II fellow pilots. Their message on a white ribbon among the leaves was "Happy Landing Eddie."

We were all there. Emma, our old cook, came from Chicago. Mother, Dad, Ninette, and Harry flew up from New Orleans. It was the first time Mother had ever flown. She had always said she was terrified of airplanes and would never fly, but for her Ned she forgot her fears. She lived exactly ten years longer, dying just short of her ninety-seventh birthday in 1985. Dad had died four years after Ned, just short of his ninety-sixth birthday.

If genetics is the determining factor, it is unlikely that Ned would have died so young. There had to be some other cause. I think he was simply burning the candle at both ends. It made a bright light, but it went out quickly. We miss that light.

One of the last pictures taken of Ned as he was sketching somewhere in the Caribbean

CHAPTER FIVE

❧

LIST OF BUILDINGS

DART BUILDINGS

Edward Dart was not good at record-keeping. He never, as far as anyone can tell, kept a systematic list of his work, nor did he routinely keep copies of his drawings and plans. Some survive; some don't. Hence the information that follows was pieced together from many sources and with the help of many people.

This list includes only buildings that he designed from scratch and only work that was actually completed. It does not include any remodeling jobs, additions, or projects that never got off the ground.

ALPHABETICAL LIST

Date indicates year (or in a few cases approximate year) of completion.

A

All Saints Lutheran Church (1962)
Louis Ancel house (1961)
George R. Anderson house (1961)
Area Six District Police Center (1972)
Milton K. Arenberg house (1956)
Augustana Lutheran Church (1967)
Evan L. Ausman house (1957)

B

Arthur Baker house (1956)
George M. Bard II house (1954)
Henry K. Beard house (1954)
William H. Bingham house (1954)
Blue Island Police Headquarters (1971)
Alex M. Buchholz house (1956)

C

Calvary Evangelical Lutheran Church (1962)
Caleb H. Canby III house (1954)
Cancer Treatment Institute, King Faisal Hospital (1981)
Catholic Churches:
  Holy Ghost Catholic Church (1967)

St. John of the Cross Church (1977)
St. Procopius Abbey Church and Monastery (1967)
Irving Cherry house (1964)
Chicago Theological Seminary faculty housing (1962)
Church of the Holy Family (1959)
George Clements house (1957)
Clock Tower Inn Resort and Conference Center (1966)
Barry Crown house (1963)

D

Edward D. Dart house (1951)
Edward D. Dart house (1956)
Edward D. Dart house (1964)
Henry P. Dart, Jr. house (1949)
Louis Degen house (1968)

E

Emmanuel Presbyterian Church (1963)
Episcopal Church of the Resurrection (1963)
Episcopal Churches:
  Church of the Holy Family (1959)

Methodist Church:
St. Luke's Methodist Church (1965)
Michael Reese Hospital (*see* Klein-Kunstadter 1970)
Midway Studios Gallery (1972)
Norman Miller house (1956)

N

Nathaniel Leverone Hall (1971)
Norris University Center (1971)
Northgate 21 House (1953)

O

John A. Orb house (1956)

P

David B. Peck III house (1957)
Petranek Drugs (1955)
Pick-Staiger Concert Hall (1969)
Pickwick Place (1955)
Pool house, Barrington, Illinois (1955)
Presbyterian Church, La Porte, Indiana (1968)
Presbyterian Churches:
Emmanuel Presbyterian Church (1963)
Lansing Presbyterian Church (1961)
Presbyterian Church, La Porte, Indiana (1968)
Public Parking Garage, Evanston, Illinois (1966)

R

Robert J. Reynolds house (1958)
Laura Rosenberg house (1961)

S

St. Ambrose Episcopal Church (1959)
St. Augustine's Episcopal Church, Benton Harbor, Michigan (1962)
St. Augustine's Episcopal Church, Gary, Indiana (1958)

St. John of the Cross Church (1977)
St. Luke's Methodist Church (1965)
St. Mark's Lutheran Church (1959)
St. Matthew United Church of Christ (1962)
St. Michael's Episcopal Church (1953)
St. Michael's Episcopal Rectory (1959)
St. Nicholas Episcopal Church (1963)
St. Procopius Abbey Church and Monastery (1967)
Samsonite Corporation Office Building (1969)
Donald J. Sersen house (1958)
Service School Barracks, Great Lakes (1968)
James M. Simmen house (1962)
Sports Center, Lake Forest College (1965)
Philip Stewart house (1953)
William Swartz house (1961)

T

Ted's Restaurant and Lounge (1955)
John E. Test house (1954)
Thornridge United Church of Christ (1961)

U

United Church of Christ Churches:
St. Matthew United Church of Christ (1962)
Thornridge United Church of Christ (1961)
United Parcel Service (1963)
University of Illinois Medical Center Administrative Office Building (1968)

V

Theodore W. Van Zelst house (1962)
Veranda House (1960)
Village Hall, Barrington Hills, Illinois (1961)

W

Water Tower Place (1976)
B. L. Webb house (1959)
Charles T. Wegner III house (1962)
Erskine Wilder house (1959)

CHRONOLOGICAL LIST

Whenever possible the pictures show the buildings as they were originally, but it must be emphasized that many of the buildings have been neglected, or added on to, or remodeled. In some cases they have been distorted beyond recognition.

If an address, picture, or the name of the present owner is missing, it is because it was unavailable or was omitted at the owner's request.

1949

Henry P. Dart, Jr. house
Godfrey Road
Thetford, Vermont

1992 owner: Doris Lingelbach

1950

John O. Karstrom, Jr. house
1300 North Waukegan Road
Lake Forest, Illinois

1992 owners: Mr. & Mrs. Richard Bobbe

1951

Edward D. Dart house
Braeburn Lane
(formerly Spring Creek Road)
Barrington, Illinois

1992 owners: Mr. & Mrs. Robert Wetzel

(1951)

Interstate Electric Supply Company
1020 Greenwood Avenue
Waukegan, Illinois
(1992 photo)

1953

George D. Lawrence house
Hills and Dales Road
Barrington, Illinois   *(1992 photos)*

1992 owner: Mrs. Wendell Fentress

Joseph J. Lucas house
701 Euclid Avenue
Highland Park, Illinois

Addition by Dart 1958
(Joseph J. Lucas photo, 1992)

1992 owners:
Mr. & Mrs. Joseph J. Lucas

(1953)

Northgate 21 House
A design project for
realtor/builder Graeme Stewart.
Several of these houses were built in
and around Wheaton, Illinois.

816 West Elm Street
Wheaton, Illinois
(1969 photo)

1992 owner: Warren K. Parent

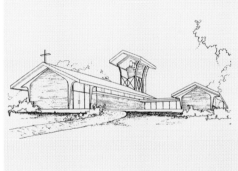

St. Michael's Episcopal Church
647 Dundee Avenue
Barrington, Illinois
(Additions by Dart
1959, 1961, 1969, 1972)

(Kranzten photo)

(1953)

Philip Stewart house
1300 North Waukegan Road
Lake Forest, Illinois

1992 owners: Mr. & Mrs. John Lillard

1954

George M. Bard II house
300 Ridge Road
Barrington, Illinois
(Marilyn Weidler photo, 1992)

1992 owners: John & Marilyn Weidler

(1954)

Henry K. Beard house
49 Hawthorne Road
Barrington, Illinois
(Torkel Korling photo)

1992 owner:
Mrs. Henry K. Beard

William H. Bingham house
Bateman Circle
Barrington, Illinois

1992 owners:
Mr. & Mrs. William H. Bingham

Caleb H. Canby III house
135 Tower Road
Barrington, Illinois

Addition by Dart 1961
(Sylvia Preston photo, 1992)

1992 owners: James & Candace Pike

(1954)

Hough Manor Apartments
620 Hough Street
Barrington, Illinois
(Sylvia Preston photo, 1992)

Robert Hunker house
Spring Creek Road
Barrington, Illinois
Demolished 1980s
(Komechak photo, 1964)

Harry G. Meadows house
Sleepy Hollow Road
Dundee, Illinois

John E. Test house
Sleepy Hollow Road
Dundee, Illinois

1955

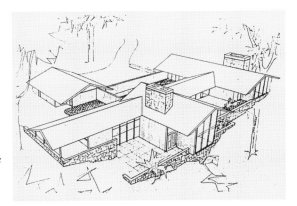

Livingston Fairbank, Jr. house
210 North Mayflower Road
Lake Forest, Illinois

D. Wendell Fentress house
77 Spring Creek Road
Barrington, Illinois

1992 owners:
Mr. & Mrs. Roger Weston

Lawrence Galloway house
Helm Road
Barrington, Illinois
(Sylvia Preston photo, 1992)

1992 owners:
Mr. & Mrs. Lawrence H. Galloway

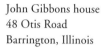
(1955)

John Gibbons house
48 Otis Road
Barrington, Illinois

1992 owners:
 Mr. & Mrs. Kenneth Ryan

Arthur R. Lutz house
247 West Lake Shore Drive
Tower Lakes
Barrington, Illinois

1992 owners: Robert & Sherry VanOchten

(Sylvia Preston photo, 1992)

(1955)

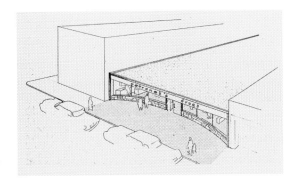

Petranek Drugs
426 North Milwaukee Avenue
Libertyville, Illinois

Pickwick Place
(A large complex of town houses)
Bristol Drive and Concord Lane
Barrington, Illinois

Pool house
North Park
Barrington, Illinois

(1955)

Ted's Restaurant and Lounge
(now Madison Avenue
Fine Dining and Spirits)
34 North Sheridan Road
Waukegan, Illinois

1956

Milton K. Arenberg house
1880 Crescent Lane
Highland Park, Illinois

1992 owners:
Mr. & Mrs. Martin Snitzer

Arthur Baker house
4 Graymoor Lane
Olympia Fields, Illinois
(Deborah Halliday photos, 1993)

1992 owners:
Mr. & Mrs. Gary Rautenstrauch

(1956)

Alex M. Buchholz house
98 Graymoor Lane
Olympia Fields, Illinois

(John MacGaw photo, 1992)

1992 owners:
Dr. & Mrs. Lawrence Chapman

(Jonathan Scott photo)

Edward D. Dart house
239 Oak Knoll Road
Barrington, Illinois

1992 owners:
Mr. & Mrs. John F. Palumbo

(1956)

Norman Miller house
27 Graymoor Lane
Olympia Fields, Illinois
(John MacGaw photo, 1992)

1992 owners: Dr. & Mrs. Howard Zeiger

John A. Orb house
46 Brinker Road
Barrington, Illinois

1992 owners: Debra & John Hilton

Lions Memorial Park pool house
Mount Prospect, Illinois
Demolished 1980s

1957

Evan L. Ausman house
153 Oak Terrace
Lake Bluff, Illinois

1992 owners:
Dr. & Mrs. Jesse K. Wheeler

George Clements house
34 Breakenridge Farm Road
Oak Brook, Illinois
(Don Honick photo)

1992 owner: Regina Halama

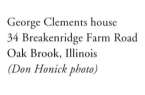

Harold M. Flanzer house
972 Sunset Road
Winnetka,Illinois
(Claude Peck photos, 1992)

1992 owner: Mrs. Harold M. Flanzer

(1957)

Elmer Johnson house
10517 South Seeley Avenue
Chicago, Illinois

1992 owners: Elmer & Elizabeth Johnson

David B. Peck III house
334 South Circle Lane
Lake Forest, Illinois

1992 owners:
Mr. & Mrs. David B. Peck III

1958

John McCutcheon house
281 West Laurel Avenue
Lake Forest, Illinois
Demolished 1992

Robert J. Reynolds house
Highland Park, Illinois
(Richard Cutler photo, 1992)

1992 owners: Mr. & Mrs. Robert J. Reynolds

(1958)

St. Augustine's Episcopal Church
1901 Ellsworth Street
Gary, Indiana
(Paul Meyers photo)

Donald J. Sersen house
825 Lill Street
Barrington, Illinois
(Donald J. Sersen photo, 1992)

1992 owners: Mr. & Mrs. Donald J. Sersen

1959

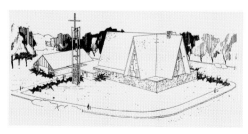

Church of the Holy Family
Sauk Trail and Orchard Drive
Park Forest, Illinois
(Ken Miles photo, 1992)

(1959)

Jules Ladany house
180 Ravine Drive
Highland Park, Illinois

1992 owner:
Ruth Ladany Eisenberg

Lutheran Church of Atonement
909 East Main Street
Barrington, Illinois

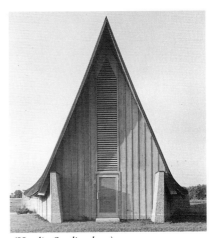

(Herrlin Studio photo)

St. Ambrose Episcopal Church
MacArthur Drive at 10th Street
Chicago Heights, Illinois
(Komechak photo)

(1959)

St. Mark's Lutheran Church
31 South Edgelawn Drive
Aurora, Illinois

B. L. Webb house
241 Oak Knoll Road
Barrington, Illinois
(Sylvia Preston photo, 1992)

1992 owners: Susan Jo Hanson & John F. Palumbo

Erskine Wilder house   St. Michael's Episcopal Rectory
Helm Road   208 West Lake Avenue
Barrington, Illinois   Barrington, Illinois
Demolished 1992

1960

Hershey house
687 Birch Lane
Glencoe, Illinois
(Richard Cutler photo, 1992)

1992 owner: Constance Hershey

Veranda House
(A spec house by an
unidentified builder who called
it Veranda House because of
the open porch in front)
Barrington Bourne
Barrington, Illinois

1961

Louis Ancel house
Glencoe, Illinois

1992 owner: Mrs. Louis Ancel

George R. Anderson house
705 Woodmere Lane
Glenview, Illinois

1992 owner: Milada Anderson

Grace Lutheran Church
950 South York Road
Bensenville, Illinois

(1961)

Walter E. Heller house
799 Highland Place
Highland Park, Illinois

1992 owners:
Mr. & Mrs. Burt Chudacoff

(Komechak photo)

Illinois Credit Union League
1035 South York Road
Bensenville, Illinois

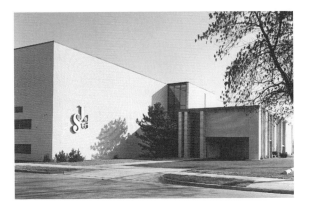

Jel Sert Company
25th Avenue
and Madison Street
Bellwood, Illinois

(1961)

Lansing Presbyterian Church
2525 Ridge Road
Lansing, Illinois
(Komechak photo)

Laura Rosenberg house
Highland Park, Illinois

1992 owners:
Arnold & Gail Heltzer

(1961)

William Swartz house
195 Ivy Lane
Highland Park, Illinois

1992 owner: Mary Swartz

Thornridge United Church
of Christ
1130 East 154th Street
South Holland, Illinois
(Ken Miles photo, 1992)

Village Hall
112 Algonquin Road
Barrington Hills, Illinois
(Richard Cutler photo)

1962

All Saints Lutheran Church
13350 LaGrange Road
Orland Park, Illinois
(Komechak photo)

Calvary Evangelical
Lutheran Church
11249 South Spaulding Avenue
Chicago, Illinois
(Komechak photo)

Chicago Theological Seminary
Faculty Housing
58th and Dorchester Avenue
Chicago, Illinois

(1962)

W. Brooke Fox house
42 Colony Road
Timberlane Estates
Gretna, Louisiana

1992 owners:
Mr. & Mrs. William P. McCord

Richard E. Henrich house
24 Brinker Road
Barrington, Illinois

1992 owners: Giacomo & Bere Antonini

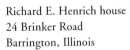

(1962)

Donald Kozoll house
465 Lakeside Terrace
Glencoe, Illinois

1992 owners: Walter & Karla Goldschmidt

St. Augustine's Episcopal
Church
1753 Union Street
Benton Harbor, Michigan
(Komechak photo)

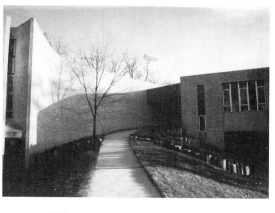

St. Matthew United Church
of Christ
25 West 360 South Gables Blvd.
Wheaton, Illinois
(Komechak photo)

(1962)

James M. Simmen house
694 East Grandview
Lake Forest, Illinois
(Jana Brinton photo)

1992 owner:
Patricia A. Minicucci

(Richard Cutler photo)

Theodore W. Van Zelst house
1213 Wagner Road
Glenview, Illinois

1922 owners:
Mr. & Mrs. Theodore W. Van Zelst

Charles T. Wegner III house
2 Lochinvar Lane
Oak Brook, Illinois
(Richard Cutler photos)

1992 owner: Joan M. Wegner

1963

Barry Crown house
350 Sunrise Circle
Glencoe, Illinois

1992 owners: Leo & Betty Melamed

Emmanuel Presbyterian Church
1850 South Racine Avenue
Chicago, Illinois
(Komechak photo)

(1963)

Episcopal Church of
the Resurrection
Route 59 and Gary Mill Road
West Chicago, Illinois
(Komechak photo)

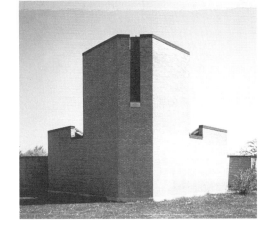

House of Prayer Lutheran Church
17450 South Crawford Avenue
Country Club Hills, Illinois
(Komechak photo)

IBM building
Western Avenue and
Bailey Streets
Sioux Falls, South Dakota

(1963)

Indian Lakes Resort Club
250 West Schick Road
Bloomingdale, Illinois
(Robert Nowell Ward photo)

Memorial Plaza and Bench
Woodberry Forest School
Woodberry Forest, Virginia
(Kenney Marlatt photo)

St. Nicholas Episcopal Church
1072 Ridge Avenue
Elk Grove Village, Illinois
(Komechak photo)

(1963)

United Parcel Service
1400 South Jefferson Street
Chicago, Illinois

1964

Irving Cherry house
Evanston, Illinois

1992 owners: Mr. & Mrs. Irving Cherry

Edward D. Dart house
66 Dundee Lane
Barrington, Illinois
(*Hedrich-Blessing/Chicago
Historical Society photo*)

1992 owner: Wilma Dart

(1964)

Holy Apostles Greek Orthodox
Church
2501 Wolf Road
Westchester, Illinois
(Komechak photo)

1965

Lorrance Academic Center
School Street and Brainard Ave.
Naperville, Illinois
(Robert Nowell Ward photo)

St. Luke's Methodist Church
100 West 86th Street
Indianapolis, Indiana
(Komechak photo)

(1965)

Sports Center
Lake Forest College
Lake Forest, Illinois

1966

Henrici's Restaurant
(now Bennigan's)
445 Skokie Boulevard
Northbrook, Illinois

Public Parking Garage
City of Evanston
Sherman Avenue
Evanston, Illinois
(Richard Cutler photo)

Clock Tower Inn Resort and Conference Center
7801 East State Street
Rockford, Illinois

1967

Augustana Lutheran Church
5500 South Woodlawn Avenue
Chicago, Illinois

First Lake County
National Bank
(now American National Bank
of Libertyville)
140 West Cook Avenue
Libertyville, Illinois
(Ezra Stoller/Esto photo, 1967)

(1 9 6 7)

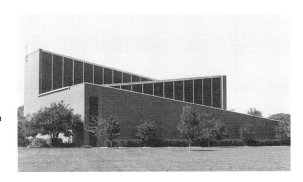

Holy Ghost Catholic Church
700 East 170th Street
South Holland, Illinois
(Ken Miles photo)

St. Procopius Abbey
Church and Monastery
5601 College Road
Lisle, Illinois
(Balthazar Korab photos)

1968

Louis Degen house
32 Polo Club Circle
Denver, Colorado
(Komechak photo)

3)

First St. Paul's Evangelical Lutheran
Church
1301 North LaSalle Street
Chicago, Illinois
(*Komechak photo*)

Lena Canada Homes
17th Street and
Greenwood Avenue
East Chicago Heights, Illinois
(*Orlando R. Cabanban photo*)

Presbyterian Church
307 Kingsbury Avenue
LaPorte, Indiana
(*Komechak photo*)

(1968)

Service School Barracks
(Dorie Miller Complex)
Naval Training Center
Great Lakes, Illinois

University of Illinois
Medical Center
Administrative Office Building
1737 West Polk Street
Chicago, Illinois
(Richard Cutler photo)

1969

Pick-Staiger Concert Hall
Northwestern University
Evanston, Illinois
(Claude Peck photo)

(1969)

Samsonite Corporation Office
Building
11200 East Forty-Fifth Avenue
Denver, Colorado
(Komechak photo)

1970

Dr. Sidney Klein Women's Hospital
533 East Twenty-Ninth Street
and
Kunstadter Children's Center
2915 South Ellis Avenue
Chicago, Illinois
(originally part of Michael Reese Hospital)

1971

Blue Island Police Headquarters
New Street and Greenwood Ave.
Blue Island, Illinois
(Komechak photo)

(1971)

Marie Skodowska Currie
High School
4959 South Archer Avenue
Chicago, Illinois

Mayer Kaplan Jewish
Community Center
5050 Church Street
Skokie, Illinois
(Richard Cutler photo)

Nathaniel Leverone Hall
Northwestern University
Evanston, Illinois

(1971)

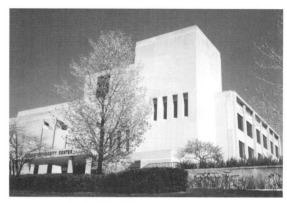

Norris University Center
Northwestern University
Evanston, Illinois

1972

Area Six District Police Center
Western and Belmont
Chicago, Illinois
(Hedrich-Blessing photo/
Chicago Historical Society
Collection)

(1972)

Midway Studios Gallery
University of Chicago
Chicago, Illinois

Completed Posthumously
1976

(Ann Duncan photo, 1992)

Water Tower Place
845 North Michigan Avenue
Chicago, Illinois

(Joseph J. Lucas photo, 1993)

Completed Posthumously
1977

St. John of the Cross Church
4920 Caroline Avenue
Western Springs, Illinois
(Balthazar Korab photo)

1981

Cancer Treatment Institute
King Faisal Specialist
Hospital and Research Centre
Riyadh, Saudi Arabia

APPENDIX

DART FAMILY TREE

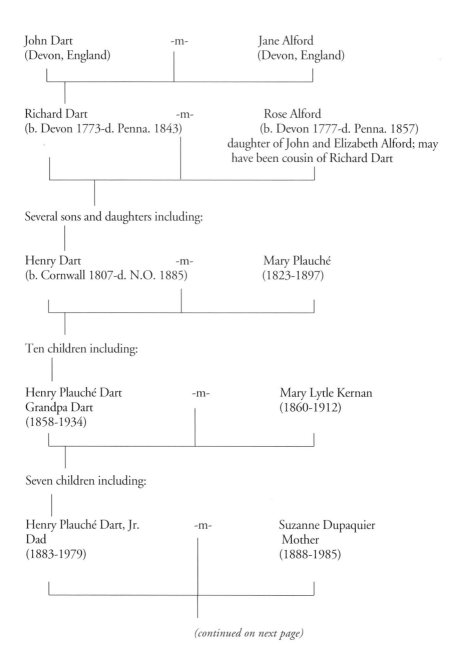

John Dart   -m-   Jane Alford
(Devon, England)   (Devon, England)

Richard Dart   -m-   Rose Alford
(b. Devon 1773-d. Penna. 1843)   (b. Devon 1777-d. Penna. 1857)
daughter of John and Elizabeth Alford; may
have been cousin of Richard Dart

Several sons and daughters including:

Henry Dart   -m-   Mary Plauché
(b. Cornwall 1807-d. N.O. 1885)   (1823-1897)

Ten children including:

Henry Plauché Dart   -m-   Mary Lytle Kernan
Grandpa Dart   (1860-1912)
(1858-1934)

Seven children including:

Henry Plauché Dart, Jr.   -m-   Suzanne Dupaquier
Dad   Mother
(1883-1979)   (1888-1985)

(continued on next page)

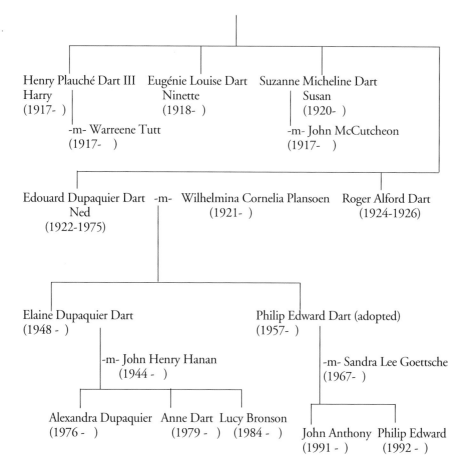

Henry Plauché Dart III   Eugénie Louise Dart   Suzanne Micheline Dart
Harry   Ninette   Susan
(1917-)   (1918-)   (1920-)

-m- Warreene Tutt   -m- John McCutcheon
(1917-)   (1917-)

Edouard Dupaquier Dart -m- Wilhelmina Cornelia Plansoen   Roger Alford Dart
Ned   (1921-)   (1924-1926)
(1922-1975)

Elaine Dupaquier Dart   Philip Edward Dart (adopted)
(1948 -)   (1957-)

-m- John Henry Hanan   -m- Sandra Lee Goettsche
(1944 -)   (1967-)

Alexandra Dupaquier Anne Dart Lucy Bronson   John Anthony Philip Edward
(1976 -)   (1979 -) (1984 -)   (1991 -)   (1992 -)

DUPAQUIER FAMILY TREE

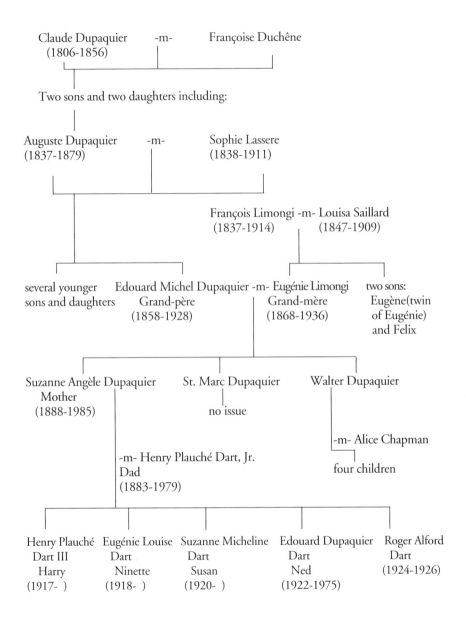

Claude Dupaquier   -m-   Françoise Duchêne
(1806-1856)

Two sons and two daughters including:

Auguste Dupaquier   -m-   Sophie Lassere
(1837-1879)   (1838-1911)

François Limongi -m- Louisa Saillard
(1837-1914)   (1847-1909)

several younger   Edouard Michel Dupaquier -m- Eugénie Limongi   two sons:
sons and daughters   Grand-père   Grand-mère   Eugène(twin
                         (1858-1928)   (1868-1936)   of Eugénie)
                                                             and Felix

Suzanne Angèle Dupaquier   St. Marc Dupaquier   Walter Dupaquier
Mother
(1888-1985)   no issue

                                                    -m- Alice Chapman
              -m- Henry Plauché Dart, Jr.
              Dad   four children
              (1883-1979)

Henry Plauché   Eugénie Louise   Suzanne Micheline   Edouard Dupaquier   Roger Alford
Dart III   Dart   Dart   Dart   Dart
Harry   Ninette   Susan   Ned   (1924-1926)
(1917-)   (1918-)   (1920-)   (1922-1975)

EDOUARD DUPAQUIER'S LETTER

New Orleans
October 2, 1886

Dear Mr. and Mrs. Limongi,

Please don't be surprised to receive this letter; there is between my family and yours a very old friendship that we, the children, have kept up. It is, therefore, very natural that we try to get closer to each other. Same tastes, same ideas; we belong to that good, hardworking bourgeois class, intelligent, thoughtful; that is to say, this bourgeoisie that leads the world today.

To this already existing sharing of values is added a personal feeling that I want you to know without further delay. Mademoiselle Eugénie has qualities that I have not often found in the numerous young ladies whose outward gaiety has caused me to be infatuated in spite of myself. These qualities are those that one seeks when one has heartfelt feelings and sound judgment, both of which I believe I have, if I may say so jokingly. Please allow me to dispense with a trite enumeration; it does not behoove me to tell you about your own daughter. We have known each other for such a short time that I dare not ask lightly today for her hand . Mademoiselle Eugénie is young. I imagine that she is going out a bit and is having a good time, but she is old enough to know her own heart and mind.

This letter is too long, I am afraid, but its goal is simply to ask your permission to know your daughter better, with all the consideration and restraint which I feel I can provide.

Should I be fortunate enough to have her find me acceptable, you can be sure that I would not delay in declaring my intentions. You can, of course, inform Mademoiselle Eugénie of my feelings, if that suits you. Thus her heart will be free and, when the time comes, if we suit each other, I believe we will not be alone in rejoicing in a good match because our families have known and liked each other for a long time. This explains why I took the liberty of speaking to you as a young friend.

Please accept my devoted and sincere feelings.

Dr. E. Dupaquier

Nouvelle-Orléans
le 2 octobre 1886

Cher Monsieur, chère Madame,
            Ne vous étonnez pas
de recevoir cette lettre; il existe entre
ma famille et la votre un
lien d'ancienne amitié que nous
avons gardée, nous les enfants—
Il est dès lors tout naturel que
nous cherchions à nous rapprocher.
Mêmes gouts, mêmes idées; nous
sommes de cette bonne classe
bourgeoise laborieuse, intelligente,
réfléchie, on peut le dire, & cette
bourgeoisie qui mène le monde
aujourd'hui.
A cette sympathie existant
déjà s'ajoute un sentiment

qui m'est personnel et
que je vous confie sans plus
tarder. Mademoiselle Eugénie
a des qualités que je n'ai pas
rencontrées souvent chez les
nombreuses jeunes filles dont l'oisi-
-veté publique a bien voulu
malgré moi me rendre passion-
-nément épris.. Ces qualités
sont celles qu'on recherche qu'aussi
on a le cœur bien placé, et le juge-
-ment sain ce que je m'accorde
volontiers, soit dit en riant —.
Permettez moi de ne pas tomber
dans une énumération banale;
ce n'est pas moi qui doive vous
faire connaître votre enfant.
Il y a trop peu de temps que
nous nous voyons pour que
je prétende à la légère vous
faire aujourd'hui une demande

en règle — Mademoiselle Eugénie
est jeune — je conçois qu'elle doive
s'amuser un peu dans le monde,
bien que d'âge à fixer son coeur et
sa raison.

Cette lettre trop longue bien malgré
moi — n'a pas d'autre but que de
demander la permission de
faire plus ample connaissance
avec votre fille, avec tous les égards
et toute la discrétion dont je me
sens capable —

Si par bonheur j'aurais à lui plaire
croyez bien que je ne serai pas
long quant à moi à me prononcer.
Avertissez d'ailleurs Mademoiselle Eugénie
si vous le voulez bien — ainsi son
coeur ne sera pas forcé et quand
il sera temps, si nous nous
agréons mutuellement — je
crois que nous ne serons

par les seuls à goûter les
joies d'une bonne alliance
car nos familles s'aiment
déjà et de longue date. Aussi
bien ai je pris la liberté
de vous parler comme un
jeune ami.

Agréez, Cher Monsieur Chère Madame
l'expression de mes sentiments
dévoués et sincères

HE'S 1-A IN THE ARMY
from the LP album,
"Praise the Lord and Pass the Ammunition"

From coast to coast in this great nation
Each man has got a classification.
Now I've got a guy who never liked to fight
But for Uncle Sam he said, "All right."
He's 1-A in the Army
And he's A-1 in my heart
He's going to help the country
That helped him to get a start.
I love him so
Because I know
He wants to do his part.
For He's 1-A in the Army
And he's A-1 in my heart.
And just in case you're quizzical
I'm gonna tell you now
He passed the toughest physical
He passed it   [words unintelligible]
For I know why he rates so high
On Uncle Sammy's chart
For he's 1-A in the Army and He's A-1 in my heart.

HIGH FLIGHT
John Gillespie Magee, Jr.

Oh! I have slipped the surly bonds of Earth
And danced the skies on laughter-silvered wings;
Sunward I've climbed, and joined the tumbling mirth
Of sun-split clouds—and done a hundred things
You have not dreamed of—wheeled and soared and swung
High in the sunlit silence. Hov'ring there,
I've chased the shouting wind along, and flung
My eager craft through footless halls of air . . . .
Up, up the long, delirious, burning blue
I've topped the wind-swept heights with easy grace,
Where never lark, or even eagle, flew;

And, while with silent, lifting mind I've trod
The high untrespassed sanctity of space,
Put out my hand, and touched the face of God.

John Magee was killed in flight training on December 11, 1941.
He was nineteen years old.

DISABLED
Wilfred Owen

He sat in a wheeled chair, waiting for dark,
And shivered in his ghastly suit of grey,
Legless, sewn short at elbow. Through the park
Voices of boys rang saddening like a hymn,
Voices of play and pleasure after day,
Till gathering sleep had mothered them from him.

About this time Town used to swing so gay
When glow-lamps budded in the light blue trees,
And girls danced lovelier as the air grew dim,—
In the old times, before he threw away his knees.
Now he will never feel again how slim
Girls waists are, or how warm their subtle hands;
All of them touch him like some queer disease.

There was an artist silly for his face,
For it was younger than his youth, last year.
Now, he is old; his back will never brace;
He's lost his color very far from here,
Poured it down shell-holes til the veins ran dry,
And half his life-time lapsed in that hot race,
And leap of purple spouted from his thigh.

One time he liked a blood-smear down his leg,
After the matches, carried shoulder-high.
It was after football, when he's drunk a peg,
He thought he'd better join.—He wonders why.
Someone had said he'd look a good in kilts,

That's why; and maybe, too, to please his Meg;
Aye, that was it, to please the giddy jilts
He asked to join. He didn't have to beg;
Smiling, they wrote his lie; aged nineteen years.
Germans he scarcely thought of; all their guilt,
And Austria's, did not move him. And no fears
Of Fear came yet. He thought of jewelled hilts
For daggers in plaid socks; of smart salutes;
And care of arms; and leave; and pay arrears;
Esprit de corps; and hints for young recruits.
And soon he was drafted out with drums and cheers.

Some cheered him home, but not as crowds cheer Goal.
Only a solemn man who brought him fruits
Thanked him; and then inquired about his soul.
Now he will spend a few sick years in Institutes,
And do what things the rules consider wise,
And take whatever pity they may dole.
Tonight he noticed how the women's eyes
Passed from him to the strong men that were whole.
How cold and late it is! Why don't they come
And put him into bed? Why don't they come?

*Wilfred Owen was killed in action in 1918 shortly after he wrote this poem.
He was twenty-five years old.*

NOTES AND SOURCES

NOTES AND SOURCES

Most of the information in this book is based on memory, on diaries I kept, or on reminiscences of family and friends. Information from other sources, unless it is clear from the text, is documented below. If a document is cited, the collection where it can be found is in parentheses.

In general, material pertaining to Edward Dart and his architecture is in Chicago, and material pertaining to the Dart and Dupaquier families is in New Orleans, housed in the following collections:

The Art Institute of Chicago (AIC)
Michigan Avenue at Adams Street
Chicago, IL 60603
(The collection consists of Edward Dart's architectural drawings and art work not destroyed, lost, or privately owned.)

Chicago Historical Society (CHS)
Clark Street at North Avenue
Chicago, IL 60614
(The collection includes Edward Dart's letters, photographs, newspaper clippings, and other memorabilia.)

Earl K. Long Library (UNO)
University of New Orleans
New Orleans, LA 70148
(The Dart collection consists chiefly of the legal papers of Henry Plauché Dart.)

Historic New Orleans Collection (HNOC)
533 Royal Street
New Orleans, LA 70130
(The collection consists of historic documents and memorabilia of the Dart and Dupaquier families.)

In addition to the collections above, the photos, notes, and documents used in preparing this book, whenever possible, have been duplicated and placed in the Edward Dart collection in the Donnelley Library of Lake Forest College, Lake Forest, IL 60045.

Chapter I
p. 9   Certificate from the Bishop of Valance. (HNOC)

p.12   French passport, dated 1853, for Claude Dupaquier, father of Auguste Dupaquier. (HNOC)

p.13   Diplôme de Docteur en Médecine, Faculté de Médecine de Paris. (HNOC)

p.14   Letter to M. and Mme. Limongi. (HNOC, also see Appendix) p.21   An 1841 journal kept by Henry Dart (father of Henry Plauché Dart) gives a good picture of his surveying work. (UNO)

p.21ff   Most of the information about Henry Plauché Dart's early life and his forebears is taken from his unpublished autobiography (copies at UNO and HNOC). His grandfather's name is given variously as Jacques Urbain Plauché and Henry Urbain Plauché (*see* autobiography; *also see* Seebold).

p.28   William Kernan Dart diary. (HNOC)

p.31   Henry Plauché Dart Jr. diary. (HNOC)

Works Consulted

Biographical and Historical Memories of Louisiana. Vol. I. Baton Rouge, 1975.

Henry P. Dart / 1858-1934, A memorial published by the Louisiana State Bar Association, Oct. 1934. (UNO, HNOC, CHS)

Garvey, Joan B. and Widmer, Mary Lou. *Beautiful Crescent / A History of New Orleans.* New Orleans, 1984.

Seebold, Herman de Bachelle. *Old Louisiana Plantation Homes and Family Trees.* Chap. XIII. Privately published, 1941.

Chapter II

All the material on Isidore Newman and the founding of the Isidore Newman School comes from a folder of papers given me by the librarian at the school in February, 1989. The items included in the folder are:

A typewritten copy of a brief biography of Isidore Newman by Eddy S. Kalin, a math teacher during the 1930s and director of the school from 1947 to 1949.

Typewritten copies of two newspaper articles on Isidore Newman from the *Times-Democrat*, February 15, 1903 and March 1, 1907.

Photocopies of three articles on Isidore Newman by Russ Greenbaum in *Community*, a publication of the Jewish Federation of Greater New Orleans (Jan. 6, 1989; Jan. 20, 1989; and Feb. 3, 1989).

Information about Edward Dart's school days at Woodberry Forest comes from reminiscences of friends and files at the school (the original letters and copy of files are at CHS).

Chapter III

Cassette tape and originals of all letters quoted are at CHS unless noted otherwise.

p.90   "High Flight" (see Appendix).

p.93   "Disabled" (see Appendix).

p.94   Dive bomber landing practice and Navy planes crashed in Lake Michigan (*see Chicago Sun Times.* Oct. 24, Oct. 28, Nov. 7, 1990). Both planes have been restored and are in the National Museum of Naval Aviation in Pensacola, Florida.

pp.94-5 H. P. Dart Jr. July 30, 1943, letter (original in Woodberry Forest School files; copy at CHS).

p.103-4 C. M. Harbison Nov. 18, 1943 letter (original in University of Virginia alumni office; copy at CHS).

p.105   USMC medical report (copy at CHS).

Works Consulted

Atlas of the Second World War. Ed. Peter Young. New York: G. P. Putnam's Sons, 1974.

Godard, Philippe. *Wallis & Futuna.* Nouméa, Nouvelle Calédonie (New Caledonia): Editions Melanesia, 1972 (republished 1991 by Editions d'Art Calédoniennes).

Grattan, C. Hartley. *The Southwest Pacific to 1900; A Modern History: Australia, New Zealand, The Islands, and Antartica.* Ann Arbor: University of Michigan Press, 1963. passim.

_____. *The Southwest Pacific since 1900; A Modern History: Australia, New Zealand, The Islands, and Antartica,* 1963. passim.

Life's Picture History of World War II. New York: Time Inc., 1950.

Naval Air Station Glenview / A Pictorial History (Bulletin put out by the Public Affairs Office, NAS, Glenview, IL 60026), no date.

Newspaper article: "Polynesian Isles Plan For Future." *New York Times.* Sat., May 11, 1963.

Oceania / A Regional Study. Ed. Frederica M. Bunge and Melinda W. Cook. Foreign Area Studies. The American University. U.S. Gov. Printing Office. Washington, D.C., June 1984.

Oliver, Douglas L. *The Pacific Islands.* 3rd edition. Honolulu: University of Hawaii Press, 1989.

Pratt, Fletcher. *The Compact History of the United States Navy.* New York, 1957. p. 217 ff.

Chapter IV

p.162   Lines quoted are from the poem "Dover Beach" by Matthew Arnold.

p.181   Harry Weese. Nov. 29, 1971, letter (CHS).

p.181   Cuscaden, Rob. First quotation: *Chicago Sun-Times.* June 24, 1973 (secttion 1-B); Second quotation: *Chicago* [magazine]. July 1977. p. 99.

p.181   Miller, Nory. *The Architectural Forum*, Jan.-Feb. 1974. pp. 44-55.

p.181-4 Quotations of Paul Goldberger, M. W. Newman, Donald Hackl, and Carl Condit: *Chicago* [magazine], July 1977. pp. 99-125.

p.184   Gapp, Paul. *Chicago Tribune,* "Arts & Fun," Nov. 30, 1975. p. 2 (section 6).

p.184   *The Sky's the Limit / A Century of Chicago Skyscrapers.* Ed. Pauline A. Saliga. New York: Rizzoli, 1990. p. 229.

INDEX